W9-AKS-865

Marlene Dietrich

MARLENE
DIETRICH

by
Sheridan Morley

McGRAW-HILL BOOK COMPANY
New York   St. Louis   San Francisco
Düsseldorf   Mexico

FOR MARGARET
WHO'S NEVER MUCH CARED FOR HER
AND FOR THE REST OF US
WHO ALWAYS HAVE

Other books by Sheridan Morley
A Talent to Amuse
Review Copies

Library of Congress Cataloging in Publication Data
Morley, Sheridan, 1941–
   Marlene Dietrich.

   Bibliography: p.
   Includes index.
   1. Dietrich, Marlene, 1904–   2. Entertainers–
Biography.
PN2658.D5M6   1977   791.43′028′0924 [B]   76–43087
ISBN 0–07–043147–7

First published in Great Britain, 1976
by Elm Tree Books/Hamish Hamilton Ltd
90 Great Russell Street London WC1B 3PT

Filmset by BAS Printers Limited, Wallop, Hampshire
Printed in Great Britain by Ebenezer Baylis and Son Ltd.,
The Trinity Press, Worcester, and London

Published in the United States by McGraw-Hill
Book Company 1977

Acknowledgements

The author and publishers wish to thank the following for permission to reproduce copyright material in this volume. For photographs: Associated Press; Cinema Bookshop; Homer Dickens Collection; Edinburgh Festival Press Office; Ronald Grant; Keystone Press Agency; Kobal Collection; London Express and News Features; National Film Archive; Popperfoto; *Punch*; United Artists Corporation; United Press International. For extracts from books and lyrics: page 7, from 'Not Yet the Dodo', published by William Heinemann Ltd, 1967 and Doubleday & Co, Inc., reproduced by permission of the Noël Coward Estate; pages 23–6, from *The Blue Angel*, Lorrimer Publishing Ltd; page 31, from *From Caligari to Hitler*, the estate of Elizabeth Kracauer; pages 31–2, from *Fun in a Chinese Laundry*, Martin Secker & Warburg Ltd and the Josef von Sternberg Estate; page 32, from *The Great Films*, G. P. Putnam's Sons, all rights reserved; pages 42 and 51, from *The Films of Josef von Sternberg* by Andrew Sarris, Museum of Modern Art Publications; page 74, from *The Moon's A Balloon*, Hamish Hamilton Ltd and G. P. Putnam's Sons; pages 74–9, from *Memo from David O. Selznick*, Macmillan London Ltd; pages 79–82, from *The Pleasure Dome*, Martin Secker & Warburg Ltd and Simon & Schuster, Inc.; pages 89–91, from *All My Yesterdays*, W. H. Allen & Co. Ltd

For full publishing details, see Bibliography.

Every effort has been made to trace the copyright holders of the photographs and quoted material. Should there be any omissions in this respect, we apologise and shall be pleased to make the appropriate acknowledgement in future editions.

'. . . our legendary, lovely Marlene'—Noël Coward greeting Dietrich at Heathrow Airport prior to her Café de Paris appearance

1

Though we all might enjoy
Seeing Helen of Troy
As a gay cabaret entertainer,
I doubt that she could
Be one quarter as good
As our legendary, lovely Marlene

THUS NOËL COWARD, introducing Marlene Dietrich to a Café de Paris audience in London during the summer of 1954. Dietrich was then already fifty-two (suggested birth dates had ranged from 1894 through to 1912 until an East German clerk located and somewhat tactlessly published an entry in his Registry detailing the birth of one Maria Magdalene Dietrich on 27 December 1901, in the Berlin suburb of Schöneberg) and at the time of her Café season she was well into a cabaret career which was to take her far away from the pre-war Hollywood in which she had made her first starring reputation.

The Dietrich of the post-war years has been first and foremost a stage figure, arguably indeed the greatest feat of theatrical engineering since the invention of the trap door; and despite the continued existence on celluloid of almost all her pre-war work it is, I believe, in solo cabaret that most of us now think of her first.

The 'Marlene' of the 1930s, a German–American creation of Josef von Sternberg and some excellent lighting cameramen, was translated by and during the war into 'Dietrich', an infinitely tougher and lonelier figure who, travelling the world on first troop and then concert tours, had learnt the greatest of all theatrical lessons: waste nothing. Money, time and herself have all been exquisitely preserved against need, and although cold to frosty before the footlights she has passed again and again the final test of stardom—the ability not just to do something, but to stand there.

Anyone who can collect, as I saw her do at a matinée one wet Saturday afternoon in 1972, a standing ovation and enough flowers to run her own Interflora must have something denied to other mortal entertainers: the question is what, and it's not a question immediately resolved by her first appearance at the front of a briskly functional orchestra. There she stands, an old and defiant German lady with a slight limp, swathed in acres of white fur, coolly receiving applause . . . sifting and apparently checking it for volume and duration, receiving it as a sovereign right with no element of mock surprise or humility in her manner. It is patently not wonderful for her to see us, or to be in our wonderful country again, and mercifully she doesn't bother even to go through the motions of telling us that it is. Hers must be one of the most icily unsentimental performances ever offered to a paying audience, and it remains absolutely unforgettable.

Conjuring out of nowhere a kind of theatrical magic which has little to do with age or reality but everything to do with stardom, Dietrich makes blurb writers of us all: to attempt a description of her in performance is to admit the existence of theatrical illusion. If you believe that the theatre is or ever could be solely about writers or directors or designers rather than performers then she is not for you: her stage presence is a constant reminder of what can be done by the chemistry of the human spirit alone. Dietrich is a musical Mother Courage, owing nothing to anyone except possibly the operator of a single dazzling spotlight with which she carries on a perpetual and exclusive love affair.

She belongs (with Lenya and Coward and Garland and Piaf and maybe now Streisand and Minnelli) to that exclusive group of singers who demand to be treated and judged theatrically rather than musically. Like Lenya she looks as though she was trained in a school of asexual teutonic drum-majors; like Coward she puts a premium on crisp diction; like Garland she can suddenly find a catch in her voice which is nothing short of heartbreaking; like Piaf she knows precisely how slowly a stage can be traversed; and like Streisand and Minnelli but none of the others she remains (or at least she did until a recent fall from an Australian stage put her, I suspect temporarily, out of action) a great working star.

There is a theory that Dietrich has grandchildren and neighbours and a passion for cleaning the houses of her closer friends; I prefer to think of her as a being from some other planet, about as closely related to the human race as Titania or Peter Pan.

Her cabaret repertoire remains curiously unchanging ('La Vie en Rose', 'Lili Marlene', 'Laziest Gal in Town', 'Lola', 'Falling in Love Again') and it is still interspersed with those vaguely autobiographical murmurings in which the late Richard Tauber is credited as 'a great friend and a great musician' and 'Lili Marlene' is preceded by a kind of wartime travelogue.

But to judge Dietrich by her repertoire is like judging Olivier by his ability to wear false noses; presence is what she is all about, and it is a formidable one. Having her sing to you is not unlike having the Statue of Liberty sing to you; her gestures are frozen, her complexion looks as though someone has sculpted it out of eggshells, and her lighting (in latter years the masterwork of Joe Davis) has all the amber reverence accorded by the Louvre to the Venus de Milo.

Survival, too, is what Dietrich is about and the notion is etched across her face in letters of alabaster: for better and for worse she has endured, and although the closing words of her act are the inevitable 'I just can't help it' from 'Falling in Love Again', the act is in fact about the very opposite of passive submission. At her considerable best, in the songs of war and despair, there is a terrible strength to her voice—a

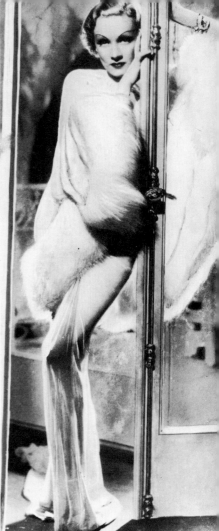

blinding emotional force that is suddenly unleashed, used, and returned equally abruptly to whatever depth of her soul it came from. I know of no voice so instantly recognisable, so immediately evocative and so quintessentially theatrical. After a swift ninety minutes in her presence one leaves the theatre having seen greatness and some of the finest curtain calls in the business, and I write of her now in the belief that there may still be somebody somewhere who has not actually seen Dietrich and does not know what he or she has missed.

Her film presence is, as we shall see later, attributable to the work of many skilled technicians—men like Sternberg and Lee Garmes who recognised in the girl from *The Blue Angel* a talent they could arrange, light and immortalise in countless soft-focus epics of the 1930s. Her stage presence is however something altogether different and entirely of her own making: while Dietrich's Hollywood contemporaries drifted into elegant post-war obscurity or tried desperately to retain

their film stardom through middle age and the increasing indignity of
supporting roles, Dietrich took herself into the theatre—there to
become not an actress, nor precisely a singer, but simply a solo star,
able to command a minimum of five thousand dollars a week for an
appearance which was to become one of the great recurring theatrical
happenings of the 1950s and 1960s.

On stage, her presence demands comparison with that of Olivier or
Barrault rather than that of any singer: there is an animal magnetism
about her, an awareness that it is not enough just to sing. Indeed the
importance of songwriters in her recital is roughly akin to the
importance of Shakespeare in Olivier's 'Othello'—a basis on which to
build. Understandably, therefore, the great songwriters have shied
away, leaving Dietrich's repertoire with very little of Cole Porter or
George Gershwin or Irving Berlin but a great deal of Friedrich
Hollander, the German composer who wrote 'Jonny' and 'Lola' and

11

With Jean Cocteau at the Theatre De l'Etoile in Paris

Edinburgh Festival, 1965: The wisest girl on earth

'The Boys in the Back Room' (this last with Frank Loesser) and who had taken the trouble to write the kind of half-spoken, half-sung material that Dietrich needed. By the same token her songs are rarely any good for anyone else to sing, and even those she has adopted from other singer/composers ('I Wish You Love' from Charles Trenet, 'La Vie en Rose' from Edith Piaf, 'Marie Marie' from Gilbert Bécaud) have somehow become more hers than theirs.

She is, then, a loner: to see her in performance is to see one of the main technical showbusiness feats of our century, and like all great conjuring tricks Dietrich is largely inexplicable. She is not by any usual standards a great singer, nor is she a great actress, nor even a great beauty; what she trades in is star quality and her use of it has caused a large number of distinguished writers to go overboard. Jean Cocteau, for instance, for whom she once sat: 'an exciting and terrifying woman' he acknowledged, 'Your name, at first the sound of a caress, becomes the crack of a whip. . . . Your beauty is its own poet, its own praise'. Kenneth Tynan claims that 'some trace of ancient Teutonic folk wisdom—many would call it witchcraft—still adheres to her. For example, she can predict a child's sex before its birth. This must of course be inspired guesswork or shrewdly applied psychology. She calls it science, as any witch would'.

More plausibly, Tynan also reckons that she was the only woman allowed to attend the annual pre-war Berlin ball for male transvestites, and there is something about her stage presence which has indeed always had an equal attraction for both sexes. Of how many other female singers can it be said that they look just as attractive in male clothing?

Dietrich is then a phenomenon, one that is unlikely to occur again; having invented herself as a stage figure (an invention which came only after a decade in which she had been all too clearly the Hollywood invention of somebody else) she proceeded to market herself around the world until she reached the 1964 Edinburgh International Festival.

Seeing her there for the first time was one of the great theatrical happenings of my life; a late-night show in which for ninety uninterrupted minutes (backed by the orchestra of Burt Bacharach to whose arrangements her post-war career owes so much) she worked her way through all the standards from the Hollywood years, turning apparently bland lyrics into erotic invitations ('They call me naughty Lola/The wisest girl on earth/At home my pianola/Is played for all it's worth') or love songs for children ('I wish you bluebirds in the Spring/To give your heart a song to sing/And then a kiss/But more than this/I wish you love') or laments for lost freedom ('Marie Marie') or lost love ('Go away, way, way from my bedside,/And bother me no more') in what must rank in the memory as one of the great sustained dramatic performances of all time.

But Dietrich is not everybody's singer and it is sometimes harder now to separate the applause for the reality of what she is doing from applause for the memory of what she has done; her records only really work as reminders of a performance which has to be seen, perhaps had to be seen, at its height—and yet I suspect that few of those who were there that night in Edinburgh, or on any one of a thousand other nights across thirty years and five continents, will ever really forget what it was like to see Dietrich work.

That, then, is Dietrich in the theatre—which is after all where she first started in the Berlin of 1922 as an actress; but her contemporary stage presence is an amalgam of technique, timing and talent much of it acquired in America immediately before and after the last war and before the legendary image becomes all-pervasive ('that Kraut', admitted Hemingway with his customarily elegant turn of phrase, 'is the best that ever came into the ring') it might be as well to go back to the very beginning and sort out a few of the facts.

2

'Look me over closely
Tell me what you see . . .'

DIETRICH HERSELF HAS never been the
most loquacious of interviewees ('I was born in Germany', she once
confided to me, 'and after I was in a film called *The Blue Angel* Mr von
Sternberg took me to America') but some painstaking research by
Homer Dickens and others has established beyond reasonable doubt
that she was the second daughter of Louis Erich Otto Dietrich, an
officer in the Royal Prussian Police, and Wilhelmina Elisabeth
Josephine Felsing who came from a well-known family of Berlin
jewellers. Maria Magdalene ('Marlene' was a contraction of the first
and last syllables in those Christian names, and came several years
later) had a governess and started life against a background of
financial and social respectability—her family was neither very rich
nor very poor but they were, in an English definition of the period,
'comfortably off'.

A year or two after her birth the family moved to Weimar and there,
soon after her father died, her mother married Edouard von Losch who
served with the Grenadiers and gave Dietrich another surname,
thereby further confusing early accounts of her childhood. In some of
these her true father is moved from the police to the (presumably more
glamorous) hussars, while others kill him off within weeks of
Dietrich's birth. In any event, his two daughters were brought up by
their mother and her second husband until he too departed, killed in
action at the Russian Front during the closing months of the First
World War, leaving his widow and her daughters in severely straitened
circumstances.

Nevertheless by 1919 Dietrich's mother had her enrolled at the Berlin
Hochschule für Musik, since school-teachers seemed convinced she
had a career as a violinist. Dietrich herself, in an interview published
in a French magazine in 1931 and generally reliable, remembered:

> At sixteen I used to practise six hours a day . . . but it happened that I
> suffered a muscle damage, so that my arm couldn't be moved for a
> time. When I was finally well again, the Doctor forbade me to play
> any difficult pieces. This made a career as a concert violinist
> unthinkable and unbearable for me. I gave up completely . . . I read

One of the Thielscher Girls (left), Hamburg 1921

and read, and there was no end to the books I wanted to read. One day I came upon a section in a book by a German poet, which I found unspeakably beautiful. I read it out loud, and the music of the words made the text even more fascinating. Around that time I began to think seriously about a theatrical career, and as soon as I returned to Berlin, I tried for an audition with Reinhardt.

'Reinhardt' was of course Max Reinhardt, then running the Deutsches Theater in Berlin as well as its neighbouring drama school where students were encouraged to break away from the 'literary' tradition of the theatre and instead to work more closely with designers, costumiers, electricians and choreographers in creating a 'living' theatre which could exist in its own right away from the printed page. He was however less than immediately impressed with the girl who auditioned for him as 'Marlene Dietrich', a name she used for the first time at that audition simply because her mother had declined to have the von Losch name, with all its distinguished military connotations, linked to anything she regarded so dubiously as a theatre school.

Disappointed but not totally discouraged by her initial failure with Reinhardt, Dietrich continued to audition for other theatre companies around Berlin and eventually got her first job in the chorus line of a touring revue: its producer, Guido Theilscher, had evidently recognised the appeal of a pair of legs that were to become among the most photographed and highly-insured in the world, and it was as one of the Theilscher Girls that Dietrich made her first appearance in Hamburg towards the Christmas of 1921.

Back in Berlin early the following year, Dietrich auditioned again for Reinhardt's theatre school and this time was accepted; according, that is, to all sources save von Sternberg who noted in his autobiography: 'I was present once when she told Max Reinhardt that she had attended his school. His eyebrows did not resume their normal position for almost twenty minutes.' Small Shakespearian rôles followed, leading up to Hippolyta in *A Midsummer Night's Dream*, and it seems reasonable to assume that it was with the Deutsches Theater that she learnt once and for all the crucial importance of stage technicalities: an intense preoccupation with lighting and other production details, left by many singers to their stage management, has always characterised Dietrich's theatre work and that preoccupation must have its origins in Berlin.

But something equally important also began for Dietrich at the Deutsches Theater: money not being all that good for small-part players, and there being a large number of them in the company at any one time, it was their custom to work simultaneously at the UFA Studios about twenty miles outside the city, doing crowd scenes or small featured rôles at a time when the German cinema was in the midst of an unprecedented boom. *The Cabinet of Dr Caligari* had been released three years earlier, and the talent at UFA in the early 1920s included Emil Jannings, Conrad Veidt, Pola Negri and—among directors—Lubitsch and Lang, Murnau and Pabst.

Dietrich's first screen appearance, made during the autumn of 1922 for a film released in 1923, was as a maid in *Der Kleine Napoleon* ('The Little Napoleon') a 'non-historical comedy' about the youngest brother of the Emperor and his amorous affairs. Dietrich was billed twelfth on the cast-list and her appearance was something less than a sensation. She returned to the Theaterschüle for the winter of 1922/23, playing increasingly important parts on the main stage including a starring rôle opposite Albert Bassermann in *Der Grosse Bariton*, a part she got in the traditional romantic-biography style when another actress collapsed hours before the first performance.

Then early in 1923, another UFA director by the name of Joe May was looking for a girl to play a couple of scenes with Emil Jannings in a drama to be called *Tragödie der Liebe* ('Tragedy of Love'). May sent an assistant, Rudolf Sieber, to audition several of Reinhardt's actresses and it was Dietrich to whom he gave the part—one which, though it still failed to make her screen name, did lead to a friendship which within a year became rather more permanent. Dietrich and Sieber were married on 17 May 1924.

In many of her later interviews, and during her cabaret routines, Dietrich has always maintained that she was 'nothing in films' until

'discovered' by von Sternberg at the time of *The Blue Angel*. But in the seven years preceding that 1930 classic she had in fact made a total of seventeen pictures, and it seems wrong therefore to follow her lead in dismissing them all out of hand.

This 1923–30 period was the most geographically settled of Dietrich's professional career: commuting between Reinhardt's theatre and the UFA studios she was in almost constant work, interrupted by the birth of her only child Maria in 1925 and by several 'domestic interludes' which were photographed by Sieber and released some time later as a short second feature entitled *The Happy Mother*.

Away from home, Dietrich did *Der Mensch am Wege* ('Man by the Roadside') adapted from the Tolstoy story and directed by a young William Dieterle who, some twenty years later, was to be found in Hollywood again directing Dietrich—this time in *Kismet*. But her 'domestic interludes' around the time of Maria's birth set Dietrich's career back somewhat and in late 1925 she was to be found as little more than an extra in G. W. Pabst's *Die Freudlose Gasse* ('The Joyless Street') which starred Werner Krauss and the Swedish actress whose Hollywood supremacy Dietrich was later to challenge, Greta Garbo.

Within another twelvemonth came a featured rôle in *Manon Lescaut* and an offer from Alexander Korda, another director then at the very beginning of his career and one who was to produce Dietrich ten years later in *Knight Without Armour*. But for now, Korda's offer was a small part in *Eine Du Barry von Heute* ('A Modern Du Barry'), a film which he had built around his then wife Maria Corda. Dietrich was billed as 'Marlaine' for reasons never fully established, and this—following

Manon Lescaut—was the second of her films to be released in America where it was shown during 1928.

Another Korda film soon followed (*Madame Wünscht Keine Kinder*, 'Madame Doesn't Want Children') on which Rudolf Sieber also got work as a production assistant and the cast included a young English actor by the name of John Loder. Dietrich followed it with better parts in some low-budget thrillers and comedies before *Café Electric*, a romantic drama which she filmed in Vienna while she was starring on the stage there as Ruby, the wide-eyed chorus girl in a translation of the Philip Dunning-George Abbot New York success *Broadway*.

From there it was back again to Berlin and Max Reinhardt, who put her into a new Sternheim play, while during the day she worked on Robert Land's film *Prinzessin Olala*. Following that, in her next Reinhardt stage production *Es Liegt in der Luft* ('It's In The Air') Dietrich sang solo for the first time, an achievement she briskly followed with featured or co-starring rôles in four more German silents.

Her career was by now split in half: in the theatre, with Reinhardt's influence and encouragement, she was doing more and more classical work (including Shaw's *Misalliance* and *Back to Methuselah*) and

'Domestic Interludes' with Maria Sieber, her only child, born 1925

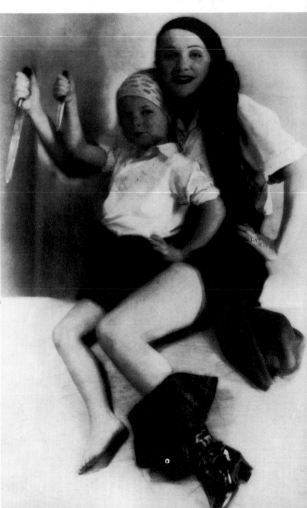

Broadway *in Vienna, 1926.*
Dietrich already approaching
centre stage: seated, second from
left

'Marlaine' Dietrich (as she was
then billed) in her first film for
Korda, Eine Du Barry Von Heute
(1926)

With Carmen Boni in Prinzessin
Olala *(1928), a romantic comedy in*
which Dietrich—with featured
billing—played the redoubtably
named Chichotte de Gastoné

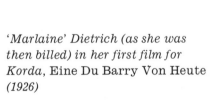

On stage (right) with Oscar Karlweiss and Margo Lion in the Max Reinhardt 1929 revue Es Liegt in der Luft

As Laurence Gerard, a young Parisienne divorcée, in Ich Küsse Ihre Hand, Madame *(1929) with her co-star Harry Liedtke (left). On the right is Richard Tauber who dubbed the title song for Liedtke. A young Fred Zinnemann was one of the assistant cameramen*

generally establishing a Berlin reputation among theatre-goers second only to that of Elisabeth Bergner who once remarked 'If I were as beautiful as Dietrich I shouldn't know what to do with my talent'; but in the cinema her talents were being confined to considerably less distinguished or demanding scripts, and it seems that Dietrich's hopes were still very firmly fixed on a stage career with the cinema at most and best a useful money-making sideline.

Louise Brooks, the silent star, took a slightly different view of Dietrich on the screen; talking about the 1929 *Ich Küsse Ihre Hand, Madame*, ('I Kiss Your Hand, Madame') she remembered, 'Her clothes were fantastic. What she couldn't wear, she carried. She was big, strong, and she naturally had the energy of a bull.'

Dietrich herself has other memories: 'Critics in Germany during the twenties always accused me of not opening my eyes enough, but I was supposed to be photogenic. In between my films I returned always to the stage. That is where Mr von Sternberg discovered me when he came to Berlin to search for a Lola for the film *The Blue Angel*.'

3

Svengali Jo

JOSEF VON STERNBERG was thirty-five when he made *The Blue Angel* in the winter of 1929–30; born in Vienna of a poor Orthodox Jewish family, he had travelled with them to New York when he was fourteen and, after a patchy education, left home to start work as an assistant film cutter before First World War service in the army got him into a training film unit alongside Wesley Ruggles and Victor Fleming. After that war, as 'Jo Sternberg', he became first an assistant and then a fully-fledged director of silents in both America and Europe. The actor Clive Brook, talking to film historian Kevin Brownlow, remembered him in 1922 standing before a mirror on a film set trying to decide whether he looked more horrible with or without a moustache 'because the only way to succeed is to make people hate you; that way they remember. . . .'

But, hated, or not, Sternberg's reputation as a director grew through the 1920s to the point where Emil Jannings actually asked him to come back from Hollywood to direct him in what was to be Jannings' first talking picture. Having left UFA in the mid-twenties to make such American films as *The Way of All Flesh* and *The Last Command*, Jannings then found his career there cut short by the coming of sound, and in 1929 he had returned to UFA in search of a suitable vehicle for a talking début in his own language. His first idea was a life of Rasputin, and he persuaded UFA's then senior producer Erich Pommer that von Sternberg was the man to direct it. Von Sternberg himself takes up the story in an introduction to *The Blue Angel* published shortly before his death in 1969:

> This German venture had a curious beginning. I had received a flattering cable from Emil Jannings asking me to guide him in his first sound film . . . this touched me deeply, as I had told him in plain language that I would not do another film with him were he the last remaining actor on earth. Once before I had directed him, in *The Last Command* . . . his behaviour interfered with everything I had planned . . . Jannings was impossible to handle. But two years had passed and bygones were bygones, or at least they should have been.
> So on, a pleasant day in August, I arrived at the Zoo Station at

Berlin to be greeted by a group containing Emil Jannings and Erich Pommer ... after a few friendly exchanges I asked what the plans were and I was told that the film I was to do was *Rasputin*. I shook my head, this failed to interest me, and I suggested that I return to the States. This caused vociferous objections, they would look around for some other idea that would provoke my interest, and I settled down comfortably in a hotel which is now razed and is a pile of rubble behind the ugly wall that divides Berlin.

In that hotel, through most of the September of 1929, von Sternberg and Jannings and Pommer discussed other possible stories; the one they eventually agreed on had first been published in Germany as a novel in 1905. It was Heinrich Mann's *Professor Unrath* and it told of a teacher who falls in love with a cabaret singer, is forced to give up his job, and at the last uses his wife's popularity to found a gambling casino where he will 'settle his score' with society and its curious moral values.

It was, to say the least, a brave choice: two years before von Sternberg arrived on that train at the Zoo Station the first Nuremberg Rally had heralded the beginning of the end of the Weimar Republic, and although in the Berlin theatre Reinhardt, Piscator and Brecht were still able to work in comparative freedom, the UFA Studios had fallen into the ownership of a right-wing industrialist called Hugenberg who must have viewed with some distrust Mann's attack on the corruption and duplicity of the German middle classes.

Still, there too a certain political freedom still obtained (Eisenstein was among the many celebrated directors working at UFA in 1929) and von Sternberg started to reshape *Professor Unrath* into the film he wanted to make—a reconstruction process in which he was aided by several draft scripts from (among others) Mann himself, Robert Liebmann, Karl Vollmöller and the playwright Carl Zuckmayer, though von Sternberg was to describe the latter's contribution as 'not worth mentioning'.

Jannings himself had recently played a series of fallen idols on the screen, dignified professional men brought down by drink or women or both, and with his cautious approval von Sternberg and the writers transformed *Professor Unrath* into *The Blue Angel*, a materially different story about a teacher (Professor Rath) falling in love with a singer (Lola-Lola) at a seedy night-club, being sacked on her account and ultimately having to work as a buffoon with her troupe before dying, alone and humiliated both sexually and socially, in his old classroom.

There remained only the problem of who was to play Lola-Lola: Brigit Helm, Trude Hesterberg, Greta Massine and Lucie Mannheim were all strong contenders for the rôle, but that was before von Sternberg first set eyes on Dietrich. Accounts of how this happened vary considerably; von Sternberg's first:

Numerous charmers were paraded in front of me. And I don't mind telling you that many of the women were extremely appealing. But they lacked *das Ewig-Weibliche*. Then on an idle evening I visited a play which contained two actors already chosen, and I noticed a woman on the stage whose face promised everything. This was Marlene Dietrich. I am credited with her discovery. This is not so. I am not an archaeologist who finds some buried bones with a pelvis that indicates a female. I am a teacher who took a beautiful woman, instructed her, presented her carefully, edited her charms, disguised her imperfections and led her to crystallise a pictorial aphrodisiac. She was a perfect medium, who with intelligence absorbed my direction, and despite her own misgivings responded to my conception of a female archetype.

Dietrich herself seems to accept that story, adding merely that when offered the rôle of Lola-Lola she told von Sternberg, 'You'd better not take me—I'm terrible in pictures.' Other versions of their first meeting suggest however that it wasn't in a theatre at all, but that she had a letter of introduction to Pommer and that it was he who took her to see von Sternberg at the UFA Studios. Either way, it worked; in von Sternberg's words 'I then put her into the crucible of my conception, blended her image to correspond with mine, and, pouring lights on her until the alchemy was complete, proceeded with a screen test. She came to life and responded to my instructions with an ease that I had never before encountered. She seemed pleased at the trouble I took with her, but she never saw the test nor ever asked to see it. Her remarkable vitality had been channelled.'

By now von Sternberg had limited the field to two: Dietrich, and Lucie Mannheim:

The two tests were screened the following morning in a crowded projection room. A unanimous opinion ruled out the woman of my choice in favour of Lucie Mannheim. I could not credit my ears, for the screen gave full proof of a unique personality. Everyone connected with the making of the film was present, and, according to a custom more prevalent, the room was also filled with others who had no knowledge of what was planned. All of them opposed my preference . . . Erich Pommer quietly settled the matter by stating that the choice of the cast was my responsibility and that it was his responsibility to support me. This of course was the final word, except for one more small voice that came from Emil Jannings who muttered in a hollow voice that would have brought credit to Cassandra that I would rue the day.

Dietrich thus became Lola-Lola: the filming of *The Blue Angel* (itself the name of the night-club where she and the Professor first meet, a mythical location after which countless real night-clubs in Paris and Berlin were soon to be named) started on 4 November 1929; it was the first sound film to be shot in Germany and a simultaneous English-language version was made. As work on the picture progressed, it became increasingly clear to Jannings that it was he rather than von Sternberg who was living to rue the day that Dietrich had been chosen: a film elaborately arranged to launch him in sound was rapidly becoming the story of a young night-club singer leading an old man to his death, and matters were not helped when Heinrich Mann told him on the set one day that the success of the film lay between the naked thighs of Miss Dietrich. It is said that such was Jannings' fury that when he came to the scene where the Professor finds Lola-Lola, now his wife, in the arms of her lover and tries to strangle her, Jannings grasped Dietrich so warmly by the throat that the marks were evident on her for several days.

Beyond doubt, and despite Jannings' efforts to restore the balance, *The Blue Angel* was to be the film that established Dietrich as an international film star and almost incidentally as a singer: her husky chanting of 'Lola' and 'Falling in Love Again' were still at the heart of her cabaret routines forty years after *The Blue Angel* was first released, and to countless film-goers the world over nothing in her career ever quite lived up to that dazzling first impression. Siegfried Kracauer

The Blue Angel: *Sternberg, Dietrich, Jannings in Lola-Lola's dressing-room*

The Blue Angel, *1930: Sternberg with Emil Jannings who had told the director he'd 'rue the day' of Dietrich's employment. In fact it was Jannings who lost most, notably his claim to solo stardom in the film*

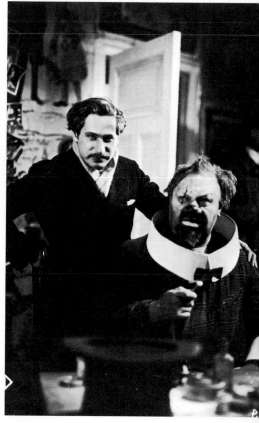

The Blue Angel: 'Dietrich's remote and fantastic creation and
Sternberg's fastidious, perverse visual texture provide a work of art
that is fascinating, narrow, unlikeable and of course flawlessly
decadent'—Gavin Lambert

summed it up in his definitive study of the German film industry *From Caligari to Hitler:*

> The film's international success can be traced to two major reasons, the first of which was decidedly Marlene Dietrich. Her Lola-Lola was a new incarnation of sex. This petty bourgeois Berlin tart, with her provocative legs and easy manners, showed an impassivity which incited one to grope for the secret behind her callous egoism and cool insolence. That such a secret existed was also intimated by her veiled voice which, when she sang about her interest in love-making and nothing else, vibrated with nostalgic reminiscences and smouldering hopes. Of course, the impassivity never subsided, and perhaps there was no secret at all. The other reason for the film's success was its outright sadism. The masses are irresistibly attracted by the spectacle of torture and humiliation, and Sternberg deepened this sadistic tendency by making Lola-Lola destroy not only Jannings himself but his entire environment.

Now, whatever you may think of Kracauer's somewhat baronial view of 'the masses' and their cinematic tastes, he has surely hit on the very essence of Dietrich's screen and later stage appeal: a secret sug-gestion, intimated but never unveiled, that there is more there than the considerable amount which already meets the eye.

Dietrich herself soon likened her relationship with von Sternberg to that of Eliza Dolittle and Henry Higgins; by all other accounts however she was (though never openly rebellious) at least thoroughly uneasy about the way the film was developing, convinced that she was wrong for the part and that the best thing she could do after its completion would be to disappear back into the theatre forever. Her singing voice also seems to have created problems, which is perhaps why the score by Friedrich Hollander and Robert Liebmann is on two or three basic notes with lyrics that can be half-spoken, half-whispered. That husky, almost mannish delivery from somewhere deep in the throat (a delivery which was to characterise all Dietrich's subsequent singing) can thus be considered to have at least a part of its origin in the UFA Studios.

In his 1965 autobiography, von Sternberg chronicled in relentless detail his relationship with an increasingly hysterical Jannings; Miss Dietrich does not however emerge from the book with very much more of the author's affection:

> She has never ceased to proclaim that I taught her everything. Among the many things I did not teach her was to be garrulous about me. . . Before becoming reconciled to being known as Marlene Dietrich, she pleaded with me to change her name, as no non-German could pronounce it correctly. The plea was ignored and she was told, correctly pronounced or not, the name would become quite well

known. She attached no value to it when I met her, nor did she attach value to anything else so far as I could ascertain, with the exception of her baby daughter, a musical saw, and some recordings by a singer called Whispering Jack Smith. She was inclined to jeer at herself and at others, though she was extremely loyal to friends (many of whom were not always loyal to her) and quick to feel pity and to help those who flattered her for qualities that were not always flattering. She was frank and outspoken to a degree that some might have termed tactless. Her personality was one of extreme sophistication and of an almost childish simplicity . . . her energy to survive and to rise above her environment must have been fantastic. She was subject to severe depressions, though these were balanced by periods of unbelievable vigor. To exhaust her was not possible: it was she who exhausted others, and with enthusiasms few were able to share. At times provoking because of her peculiar superstitions, she balanced this with uncommon good sense which approached scholarship.

That portrait of Dietrich, remembered across thirty-five years and presumably implanted in von Sternberg's mind at a time when his own ego and hers and Jannings' were on a near-collision course, lives on as one of the most detailed ever written of a lady who has not exactly encouraged exploration of her private life or temperament by others. It seems reasonable, having read it, to assume that the creation of Lola-Lola, who as much as Sally Bowles was to be forever linked with pre-war Germany (and to whom Liza Minnelli's performance in *Cabaret* surely owes a certain if secondary debt) was the result of a partnership rather than a dictatorial director and a slavish imitator. If further proof be needed, the disastrous 1959 Mai Britt/Curt Jurgens remake (without Dietrich or, admittedly, von Sternberg but with many of his original ideas) might perhaps be considered.

When the film was eventually released in America (after a delay which will be explained later) Bosley Crowther reckoned that 'in its singular contemplation of the sudden disintegration of a pillar of bourgeois society under the quick, corrosive influence of a strong application of gutter sex, it starkly reveals the imperfection and fraudulence of the façade of middle-class decency and discipline that its ponderous hero represents. It sourly suggests the soggy culture out of which Nazism oozed. And in the sadistic frenzy of the schoolboys to torment and destroy their hated teacher after they have witnessed his weakness for the cabaret girl, we may spot the incipient viciousness of later Hitler youth.'

Mr Crowther's perception was of course aided there by the wisdom of hindsight but even at the time of its first release, indeed before its first release, *The Blue Angel* caused some unease; filming was completed at UFA on 22 January 1930 and soon afterwards, seeing a rough-cut, the studio owner Hugenberg was appalled. Convinced that the character of the Professor was a crude caricature of himself, he tried to have the release date indefinitely postponed; however, half a million dollars was at stake and *Der Blaue Engel* had its world première on 1 April 1930 at the Gloria Palast Theater in Berlin. Dietrich was on stage at the end (dressed, noted von Sternberg waspishly, 'not as if she might have to sneak out of the stage door and run . . . but festooned and garlanded in the flouncy tradition of the film star') to receive a thunderous ovation.

It was, one way and another, a remarkable evening; leaving the cinema with the applause still ringing in her ears she made her way to the railroad station and there boarded the boat train for the *Bremen* and so to America where a two-film contract with Paramount awaited her. The fact that it had been signed and sealed some six weeks in advance of the world première of *The Blue Angel* was due solely to Josef von Sternberg who, immediately before shooting began, had shown the Dietrich screen test to Paramount's European representative.

The Sieber family and Sternberg (right) in Berlin at the time of The Blue Angel

4

Men cluster to me
Like moths around a flame,
And if their wings burn
I know I'm not to blame . . .

THE SUCCESS OF *The Blue Angel* in Berlin confirmed rather than created Dietrich as a star; it had after all been fully twelve months earlier, after the release of *Ich Küsse Ihre Hande, Madame* that a German illustrated magazine reached bookstalls with a diagonally divided cover featuring Dietrich and Garbo in the same sized photographs, though for Dietrich herself *The Blue Angel* was the film in which she was born: 'What about the ones you made before that?' she was once asked at a press conference, only to reply abruptly 'I made none'.

All the same, a Berlin triumph ('The Sensation: Marlene Dietrich' headlined the *Berliner Borsenkurier* the morning after the première; 'she sings and plays almost without effort, phlegmatically. But this knowing phlegmaticism excites. She does not "act" common: she is. Her performance is all cinematic, nothing is theatrical') did not necessarily mean a world-wide triumph, and though the English-language version of *The Blue Angel* was safely in the can, UFA had no plans to release it for the time being.

Paramount, moreover, in the person of B. P. Schulberg who was their general manager from 1926 to 1932, had taken a considerable risk in signing her to a two-picture contract. True, MGM had imported Greta Garbo four years earlier and were beginning now to reap the profits, but Schulberg had no way of knowing that Dietrich's sultry, rather tawdry screen image (so perfectly attuned to the Berlin of Brecht and Weill and *The Threepenny Opera* which had opened there just two years in advance of *The Blue Angel*) was going to work for an altogether different market in America. Nor did Dietrich herself view the contract with any great enthusiasm; talking in Paris to Derek Prouse thirty-four years later she recalled:

After the success of *The Blue Angel* I just went with Mr von Sternberg to America for one film—one film, and then if I didn't like the place Mr Schulberg promised I could be released. Otherwise I wouldn't have gone—I wanted nothing to do with a seven-year contract or anything like that. I had to look at the country first: I didn't know if it was good enough for my child. Then I saw it was good and I brought her over and my husband came whenever he could—he was working in Paris for Paramount around that time.

Since the contract had been a direct result of von Sternberg's enthusiasm, it was natural enough that Paramount should see him as their Mauritz Stiller to Dietrich's Garbo; there was never any doubt that he would direct her first American film, though there was some doubt about what that film would be. Sternberg himself had returned to California before *The Blue Angel* première, and seeing him off at the station Dietrich had presented him with a basket of fruit in which she'd buried, presumably not in a spirit of total disinterest, a book about Foreign Legion life called *Amy Jolly* and sub-titled *A Woman of Marrekech*. Sternberg saw in it the makings of the Hollywood film which subsequently became *Morocco*, but on the high seas aboard the *Bremen* some weeks later, Dietrich herself began to have second thoughts and cabled him protesting that the story was 'weak lemonade' and begging him to find some other vehicle for her Hollywood début. The cable also enquired, pointedly, who was to be her first American co-star.

By the time the *Bremen* docked in New York, however, there were other and more pressing problems to be sorted out; on the quayside, reports John Baxter, was one Riza Royce von Sternberg, Josef's wife, who was not there to welcome Miss Dietrich but to have her served with a writ for alienation of her husband's affections to the tune of £100,000 plus a further £20,000 for libel. The lawsuits arose out of a Viennese magazine article which quoted Dietrich saying that von Sternberg was tired of his wife and would soon be getting a divorce on her account. Paramount urged a quiet, quick settlement; Dietrich, not a compliant lady at the best of times, fought the action through its early stages until she extracted a confession from the journalist who had written the piece, that he had invented the whole story for his readers' delight.

But there were still other problems to be solved, notably how should Dietrich be sold to the Great American public? The first Paramount front-office idea was, predictably, to go with the 'Another Garbo' approach: here, after all, was yet another enigmatic European able to break men's hearts with a smile, and she too had at her side a powerful director—one who in this context soon became locally known as 'Svengali Jo'.

Garbo didn't give interviews? Neither then would Dietrich. The beginning of a $500,000 publicity campaign was marked by one simple studio handout reading:

She has fair hair with a reddish tinge, blue-green eyes and a supple figure. She looks very unlike the popular conception of a Continental. Height: 5′ 5″, Waist: 24″, Weight: 120 pounds.

Arriving in America on the Bremen, *1930*

With Sternberg in 1930, at the time when his wife was suing Dietrich for 'alienation' of her husband's affections

Visiting Chaplin on the set of his City Lights, *1930*

'Movie Classic' cover, May 1931; the Garbo/Dietrich battle already under way

S-M

MOVIE CLASSIC

MAY

10 ¢

Marlene Dietrich

MARLAND STONE

The NEW
GARBOS
of the SCREEN

LOUISE RICE
Noted Graphologist
READS Between the Lines of
DIETRICH'S Handwriting

But Adolph Zukor, then Paramount's studio head, decided that building 'a wall of inaccessibility' around Dietrich was too imitative even by Hollywood standards. To avoid rapid accusations of Garbo-mimicry he instructed Dietrich to give interviews whenever asked. At these, to the surprise of newsmen, she talked almost exclusively of her little girl back home in Germany, and did not go out of her way (as was then the custom) to endear herself to the Great American Public: 'American women', she told *Picturegoer* in May 1931, 'talk always of their jewellery. They go to parties and drink cocktails but it is all such hollow enjoyment. It makes me very miserable: I like gay people.'

Never one to suffer fools or journalists gladly (one of her more indelible traits), Dietrich also issued through Paramount a list of those subjects which bored her too much to talk about during interviews. It read: 'horse-racing, evangelism, fish, radio, police dogs, after-dinner speeches, dieting, sopranos, first nights and slang.'

She did however have an almost immediate effect on the way America dressed, as Zukor later recalled:

Marlene's indifference to publicity was a major reason why millions of Americans today wear slacks. At one point our publicity department decided that new Press photographs of Dietrich were needed. 'I'm loafing around in slacks' she told Blake McVeigh, the publicity man assigned to get the pictures. 'If you want to shoot me this way, all right.' The idea was rejected. It happened though that a little later McVeigh noticed a small display of gardening slacks for women in a Los Angeles department store. He thought, well, if even a

The Trouser Pioneer: with Groucho Marx . . . and with Chevalier and Gary Cooper at the time of Morocco *(1930)*

few women wear slacks there might be an angle in Marlene's suggestion. She posed in her trousers and, to the surprise of everybody, the photographs were in great demand by the Press. All over the country the stores were raided for their small supplies of women's slacks. The rage was on.

Meanwhile von Sternberg, undeterred by Dietrich's cable from the *Bremen*, was hurriedly putting *Amy Jolly* (about to be known once and for all as *Morocco*) into production for Paramount. The feeling around the studio was that it would be better to have Dietrich launched on America in a home-grown product and for *Morocco* and von Sternberg they pulled out all the stops: Gary Cooper to co-star, Adolphe Menjou in support, and photography by Lee Garmes.

The story, about a young cabaret singer (Dietrich) who gives up the love of a wealthy artist (Menjou) in order to follow an insouciant foreign legionnaire (Cooper) into the desert (a finale described by C. A. Lejeune in the *Observer* as 'one of the most absurd of all time') was kept to its barest essentials while Sternberg concentrated on the mood and the atmosphere of 'steamy, sultry Morocco'. The 'androgynous vision' wrote Richard Whitehall later, 'of a tuxedoed and top-hatted Dietrich chanting a little French song accompanied by highly

suggestive gestures almost qualifies it for the place of honour in an NFT season of pornographic films.'

But this was still to be America's first real look at Dietrich on screen: for *Morocco* she got an Academy Award nomination (though the Oscar went in that year to Marie Dressler) and notices to the effect that though not another Garbo she was 'a vividly beautiful young lady and an excellent actress' (*Outlook*).

The filming had not been without its problems, however, especially during the sequences for which Sternberg had Dietrich in top hat and tails:

> The formal male finery fitted her with much charm, and I not only wished to touch lightly on a Lesbian accent (no scene of mine having any sexual connotation has ever been censored) but also to demonstrate that her sensual appeal was not entirely due to the classic formation of her legs . . . at once I ran into a storm of opposition. The studio officials swore by all that was sacred that their wives wore nothing but skirts, one of them even going so far as to claim that a pair of trousers could not be lifted. Hours of debate ensued, draining my energies and theirs.

Hours were also spent trying to get Dietrich's English (or perhaps American) accent into passable condition, and the amount of time that took did not please Gary Cooper who noted of von Sternberg later 'it was bad enough not knowing what he was talking about, but I didn't even know what was going on . . . I would yawn to deliberately call attention to myself.' Observers were generally happier, though as John Baxter noted some years later 'aiming for a tropical eroticism Sternberg instead achieved a vague parlour Arabic.'

Paramount released *Morocco* with top billing for Gary Cooper, but the slogan on the posters said 'Marlene Dietrich—The Woman All Women Want To See', confidence which was not repaid by the first sneak preview at which a large number of the audience walked out on the grounds that it wasn't the new Cooper western they'd been led to expect. Reviews were however generally excellent and with *Morocco* Paramount were able to extract themselves from all their current financial difficulties. Zukor later told Sternberg that he alone had 'saved' the studio.

To the big stars of the day (Chaplin, Garbo, Swanson, Barrymore, Bow, Chevalier, Shearer and Macdonald) von Sternberg had added another: 'Dietrich is a flaming sunset' wrote a critic, while in England

Trouser-suited studies in black and white

The camp follower: Dietrich and Gary Cooper, Morocco *(1930)*

'What am I bid for my apples?' Morocco *(1930)*

James Agate added simply 'She makes Reason totter on her throne'.

Later reviews were almost as good; *Films in Review* pointed out that 'the theme of the soldier and the lady following her man into battle or wherever he goes is a familiar one but von Sternberg did it first and best'; while Pauline Kael once said she preferred the 'romantic nonsense' of *Morocco* to the 'heavy breathing' of *The Blue Angel*.

Today, Dietrich's portrayal of Amy Jolly (one of 'the legion of lost women', no less) may seem faintly disappointing after the higher definition of her *Blue Angel* performance; but what's important about this film is the way that von Sternberg, conscious of a new and less sophisticated American audience, managed to strip away the 'petty bourgeois tart' that Kracauer had seen in Dietrich's Lola-Lola and create instead an acceptable American screen image for her which Alistair Cooke once described as being of 'a beauty so overwhelming that it allows her own character never to come into play and therefore never to be called into question . . . it is because the Dietrich character has no home, no passport, no humdrum loyalties, that the memory can hold her only in permanent soft-focus.'

Night of the Locust: the Hollywood première of Morocco *at Grauman's Chinese Theatre*

Dietrich was to remain in that special Sternberg soft-focus for five more Paramount pictures in the thirties, but long after their association was broken off she maintained the 'stateless' image, describing herself in interview after interview as a kind of wandering star.

As soon as *Morocco* was in the can Dietrich returned to her husband and daughter in Berlin; by now *The Blue Angel* had made her Germany's leading box-office attraction and there were crowds to meet her at the station. In contrast, American reaction to *The Blue Angel* (released there immediately after *Morocco*) was more subdued, perhaps because audiences in the U.S. had already grown accustomed to a different, softer Marlene.

Back in Hollywood, she was greeted by a glowing review from Richard Skinner ('her work as we have now seen it in both *The Blue Angel* and *Morocco* stamps her as an actress of unusual merit') and the news from von Sternberg that they were to start work immediately on the second picture specified by their Paramount contracts.

There's no boa like the same boa: (below) Dietrich as Amy Jolly (Morocco 1930) and (left) as Lily Czepanek (Song of Songs 1933). Paramount's costume department wasted nothing

Dietrich as X-27 in Dishonoured *(1931): 'her hasty rise to film celebrity is the result of neither luck, accident nor publicity . . . her almost lyrically ironic air of detachment and her physical appeal make her one of the great personages of the local drama'—Richard Watts*

5

*'It took more than one man to change
my name to Shanghai Lily . . .'*

WHEN, SEVERAL YEARS later, James Joyce
told Dietrich that he had seen her in *The Blue Angel* she replied 'Then
Monsieur, you have seen the best of me' and it is, indeed, possible to see
in the films she made for von Sternberg in Hollywood a slow decline
from the Berlin heights. The one which followed *Morocco* was a spy
saga dreamed up by von Sternberg himself and scripted by Daniel
Rubin under the studio-inflicted title *Dishonoured*—much to the fury
of von Sternberg, who pointed out that his heroine was not to be
dishonoured but killed, and by a firing squad at that.

Dietrich played X-27, a Mata Hari of the streets who in the opening
scene is heard (conveniently by a secret agent) telling a policeman 'I
am not afraid of life—although I'm not afraid of death, either', a line
which (as Alexander Walker remarks) sounds like the translation of
some regimental motto. Thus qualified, however, she becomes a spy
and for plot reasons is soon found disguised as a peasant maid, an
identity which she said later was the only one that ever reflected her
real self on the screen.

Her co-stars in *Dishonoured* were Victor McLaglen (cast, or rather
miscast, after Gary Cooper declined the rôle on the grounds that he
had promised never to work with Dietrich again—a promise he broke
for *Desire* in 1936 by which time it was possible to work with Dietrich
without also working with von Sternberg which was, one suspects,
Cooper's real objection), Lew Cody and Warner Oland, while a smaller
part was played by Bill—later William—Powell. Of Dietrich's performance Richard Watts wrote 'she proves once more that her hasty rise
to film celebrity was the result of neither luck, accident nor publicity
. . . her almost lyrically ironic air of detachment and, to be as frank
about it as possible, her physical appeal make her one of the great
personages of the local drama.'

In other words she was, then as always, a very sexy lady and her
'local' drama was by now on screens across the world. Other critics
however remained convinced that von Sternberg was using her as box-
office bait while he pursued his determination to make visual patterns
on the screen of such beauty that what went on inside them was
irrelevant—no plot, no character seemed to matter as much to him as

the light-and-shade composition of individual set-ups and lap dissolves. And von Sternberg himself was now in some doubt as to the nature of his relationship with his star:

Again my lovely charmer, now fully established as the reigning queen of the cinema, disclaimed credit for her performance and once more this ricocheted and gained additional laurels for her, sprinkled with abuse for her director.

One of this film's final images, of 'X-27' holding up a firing squad while she fixes her lipstick, was to join a gradually increasing number of ineradicable Dietrich folk-memories, and her performance as always suggested greatness dealing with trivia. 'It is' wrote Norbert Lusk in *Photoplay* (May 1931) 'as if the Delphic Oracle had stepped down from her pedestal to give her opinion of the weather.'

Lee Garmes was again credited with the camerawork, though Dietrich later insisted that a great deal of it was done by von Sternberg himself anonymously, since he lacked the right union card. Her insistence seems wrong, however, in the light of a detailed interview given by Garmes some years later:

Dietrich always liked the north light; she had a great mechanical mind and knew the camera. She would always stop in the exact position that was right for her. Unfortunately I didn't have sufficient time to make preliminary tests with her, but I'd seen *The Blue Angel* and based on that I lit her with a side light, a half-tone, so that one half of her face was bright and the other half was in shadow. I then looked at the first day's work and I thought 'My God, I can't do this, it's exactly what Bill Daniels is doing with Garbo!' We couldn't, of course, have two Garbos! So without saying anything to Jo, I changed to the north-light effect ... the Dietrich face was my creation.

Barbara Stanwyck, Constance Bennett, Mary Pickford and Ruth Chatterton all had major pictures opening the same week as *Dishonoured* in March 1931, and within a year Garbo was to play Mata Hari; nevertheless it was Dietrich who captured the attention here, she who first immortalised the glamorous spy in talking pictures, and she who, having by now reached the end of her first Paramount contract, was able to renegotiate at a fee of $125,000 per picture.

But immediately after the completion of *Dishonoured* she returned to Germany to spend Christmas with her beloved daughter—and incidentally to promote *Morocco* on its European release. Interviewed in Berlin about her 'unusual' marriage to Sieber she replied 'When two people love each other, they should know how it is between them. I haven't a strong sense of possession towards a man. Maybe that's because I am not particularly feminine in my reactions. I never have been.'

Return to Berlin, 1931
On board ship: the Delphic Oracle
steps down
In London for a film première at
which the management said it with
flowers
At the St Lazare station in Paris
with her husband and the now
famous trousers, 1932

But this time Dietrich was determined not to leave Maria or her husband behind: Germany was already showing distinct signs of being a less than ideal country in which to spend the 1930s, anti-semitic posters were already on the streets of Berlin and when, early in the following year, Marlene returned to Hollywood and von Sternberg it was with her daughter and it was effectively forever—her husband followed them to California as soon as his European film work permitted, and Dietrich herself was only ever to return to her native land on brief post-war troop and cabaret tours.

Back in Hollywood she found that von Sternberg had completed his *An American Tragedy* and was ready to go to work with her once more: 'this time' he told a visitor to his set 'I think I will get sick and stay away and let Dietrich direct . . . some of my best ideas are hers.'

Dietrich repaid the compliment: 'Before I had my child, I stopped and looked at every child in the street. I was so crazy about all children. But now, when I have my own child, that is perfection. Why should I look at others? I feel the same way about directors. I have the best.'

Back to work at Paramount, complete with Sieber and the stellar symbol

Their new picture came about in a then-conventional way, as Dietrich later explained: 'in those days of block-booking, Paramount would often offer exhibitors 'two Marlene Dietrichs' per year before we had any idea of what they would be about, but we had to produce them on schedule just the same. More than once we were told in the middle of one picture that we must begin the next immediately after finishing the current one. In those circumstances Jo sometimes had no choice but to make up his own stories. I remember one evening after we had screened the rushes and made ready for the next day's shooting von Sternberg said 'How would you like to be a woman travelling alone from Peking to Shanghai? Perhaps we might call you Shanghai Lily . . . .'

The result, with some scripting assistance from Jules Furthman, was *Shanghai Express*, arguably the best and certainly the most profitable of all the Dietrich–Sternberg Hollywood movies: it grossed some three million dollars at a time when most ticket prices still started at ten cents, and the reason for it was undoubtedly the film's classic 'Grand Hotel on wheels' format, one which has sent train pictures roaring through to box-office records from the Shanghai to the Orient Express.

Co-starring with Dietrich was an impassive, tight-lipped Clive Brook at the head of an impressive cast-list which also featured Anna May Wong, Warner Oland and Emile Chautard, and the plot set Dietrich's now inevitable glossy tart-with-a-heart-of-steel up against Brook's implacable Englishman, a character whose final speech to her was worthy of Coward himself:

I'm not going to let you go out of my life again, Magdalen. Everything else has become so unimportant. I don't care whether you were going to leave with another man or not, nor do I want to know the reason. All I want is another chance for a new start. I'll be different. You'll never have any cause for regret. Please forgive me for my lack of faith, please do. I know I've no right to ask you even to listen to me.

Despite some unintentionally hilarious moments (like the one on the observation platform where due to some bizarre composition Brook appears to be sitting in Dietrich's lap) *Shanghai Express* survives as a thirties classic, leading Alexander Walker to suggest that the Shanghai Lily should be regarded as some kind of posthumous battle honour, awarded to those who have fought and lost Dietrich on the screen. But it was a lavish picture even for its time: thousands of Asian extras were assembled and a spur of the Santa Fe railroad closed off. Asked by Clive Brook why everyone in the film spoke in clipped, rhythmic monotones von Sternberg replied 'This is the Shanghai Express: everyone must talk like a train.'

But it is the last image that lingers: Brook, kissing Dietrich, takes

'It took more than one man to change my name to Shanghai Lily' With Clive Brook aboard Paramount's *1932* Shanghai Express

Passion and a stiff upper lip: Dietrich and Brook

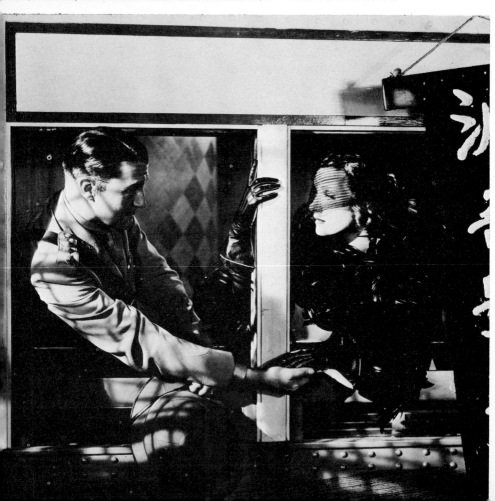

The inseparables: Sieber and Sternberg, Maria and Marlene at a Hollywood polo match, 1934

his whip and gloves and surrenders them to her: given the almost martial 'every other inch a gentleman' bearing that she and Sternberg had already established (from now on Dietrich would spend almost as much screen time in uniform as in evening dress) and the sexual power of her film presence, it too became one of the permanent fixtures in the Dietrich gallery.

Shanghai Express, its director and its cameraman (Garmes again, making the last of his Dietrich/Sternberg pictures) were all up for Oscars though only Garmes actually got one—*Grand Hotel* and Frank Borzage were the other winners.

There were by now various rumours that Dietrich and Sternberg wished to return to independent careers, and Dietrich was even tipped for the Helen Hayes rôle in *A Farewell To Arms*, but together they went straight on to *Blonde Venus* which, suggests John Kobal, was an indirect reply to other current gossip about themselves.

In the story of a woman who prefers home and child (Sieber and Maria?) to a career (Hollywood?) and a rich lover (Sternberg?) could be seen a neat parallel, though the film itself was a pretty terrible example of the then fashionable 'confessional' genre as practised elsewhere by the likes of Joan Crawford. Still, it was almost as great a

Dietrich 1931–41: a decade of hairstyles

popular success as *Shanghai Express*, though not with the London critic James Agate who wrote:

> The story begins with Dietrich pretending to be an American cabaret star, which is unthinkable. Marlene can be a star of cabaret on condition that that star is Russian or Andalusian or even Icelandic. She can never be American because the pert and the common are not in her repertoire.

So much for America; and even there the film (co-starring Herbert Marshall and a young Cary Grant) attracted some equally discouraging reviews including one from Mordaunt Hall in the *New York Times* who called it 'muddled, unimaginative and generally hopeless'. One reason for the muddle might have been differences of opinion during the shooting between von Sternberg, whose original story it again was, and Paramount who regarded the ending (in which an unfaithful wife is taken back by her ever-loving husband) as immoral. Refusing to change it, von Sternberg was suspended by the studio who reassigned the film to Richard Wallace. Dietrich however declined to work with anyone else ('Von for all' she is reputed to have cried, 'and all for Von') and after a week-long battle the two sides compromised with some minor alterations. Because of these Sternberg later disowned the film, though its highlight (a 'Hot Voodoo' dance sequence in which Dietrich emerges as the Blonde Venus from within a hairy gorilla suit) is generally reckoned to include some of his best footage, or at the very least to mark a high spot for 'Dietrich camp' followers.

6

'Jo, where are you?'

STERNBERG'S CONTRACT WITH Paramount was due to expire soon after he finished *Blonde Venus* and although he set off for Mexico in October 1932 ostensibly to shoot preliminary footage on a projected circus picture for Dietrich, there was in fact no agreement about another film at Paramount. Schulberg therefore suggested that while they were sorting out what to do next, Dietrich should try working with some other director. Sternberg agreed, and the hapless Rouben Mamoulian found himself lined up to direct her in *Song of Songs*, a 1933 remake of a story which had already been tried silently by Pola Negri and (before her) Elsie Ferguson.

As shooting was about to start Dietrich announced she would not after all be taking part; Paramount promptly sued her for $180,000 which they said was the cost of the film so far, and they also got a court injunction to stop her sailing for Germany where von Sternberg was said to be setting up his own production company.

Defeated and not exactly delighted, she went to work for Mamoulian on the uninspired account of a peasant girl who becomes first a sculptor's model, then a society lady and finally a café singer; on the set, before each take, it was rumoured that Marlene would whisper into the microphone 'Jo, where are you now that I need you?' not a question to inspire confidence in Mamoulian or her co-stars Brian Aherne and Lionel Atwill—though once the film was completed Mamoulian was able to show it to Garbo as part of his credentials for directing her in *Queen Christina*. 'Poor Mr Mamoulian', Dietrich admitted later, 'I did behave atrociously towards him ... but then I was very unhappy in the film.'

In England the *Daily Telegraph* took an equally dim view of *Song of Songs* ('Miss Dietrich's fans seem to ask nothing more than that she should be well photographed in suitable situations and unsuitable clothes') and in Germany the film was banned altogether, officially because of its 'immorality' but in fact because of Dietrich's already publicized determination never again to work in an increasingly Nazi-controlled nation.

Von Sternberg had by now returned to Hollywood, his hopes of a German production company swiftly ruined by the discovery when he

*A new director: with
Rouben Mamoulian on
the set of* Song of Songs
(1933)

arrived that Pommer and Reinhardt had already fled to London and
that UFA were about to sack all their Jewish artists. He and Dietrich
(who had herself just been through an uneasy time with a highly-
publicized but happily unsuccessful attempt to kidnap her daughter
Maria) therefore signed for two more Paramount pictures, and in an
interview at this time Dietrich explained (or went as far as she ever has
towards explaining) the basis of their unique relationship:

> I myself don't like making pictures. I can live without them. I
> haven't got to act to be happy. But I am happy with Mr von Sternberg
> because I can trust him. How do I know what another director could
> do with me? I work when Mr von Sternberg asks me to, simply
> because I know what he can do for me and with me, not because of any
> 'Svengali and Trilby' influence. I am devoted to him, but I made the
> devotion myself because my brain told me to. If you meet a great
> person you become devoted. He has no patience with stupid people.
> He has no patience with me while I am stupid. Which I understand.
> Why should he waste his time?

Dietrich's penultimate film with von Sternberg was *The Scarlet
Empress*; Garbo had done *Queen Christina* the previous year, in England
Elisabeth Bergner had just done *Catherine the Great* and there was, if
you'll forgive the idiom, a need (albeit unstated) to keep abreast. It
was of course to be a costume epic, featuring not only Dietrich but also
her daughter Maria, as well as John Lodge, Sam Jaffe, Louise Dresser
and the ever-distinguished C. Aubrey Smith. Essentially a comedy,

played out against lavish Hollywood back-drops, it seemed to suffer from an uncertainty about whether it was supposed to be history or impressionism, though Sternberg himself was in no doubt: he called it 'a relentless excursion into style' and added, lest there be any lingering doubts about whether the real Catherine II ever rode up the steps of her palace on horseback to the strains of 'The Ride of the Valkyries', 'I intend this to be not necessarily an authentic work but something beautiful to appeal to the eyes and the senses.'

Paramount, fearful of competition from Czinner's *Catherine the Great*, held up the release of *The Scarlet Empress* for eight months; even then it opened to a disastrous press and the widespread feeling that mid-1934 was not perhaps the best of economic times for a film of such lush and exotic extravagance. Critics in England were not noticeably more enthusiastic: C. A. Lejeune for the *Observer* said that Dietrich's Empress suggested at best 'a lady with a good pair of legs and few other resources at all', adding that the film itself was 'ill-mannered and lecherous'.

Critical hostility (and more importantly the failure of *The Scarlet Empress* to recoup its $900,000 costs at the box-office) coupled with the arrival at Paramount of a new star by the name of Mae West, all added up to a severe weakening of the Sternberg–Dietrich axis there. B. P. Schulberg was about to be replaced by Ernst Lubitsch as the studio's production chief, and clearly Sternberg's days were numbered. There was, however, to be one more film with Dietrich: originally called *Caprice Espagnol* but retitled *The Devil Is A Woman* on Lubitsch's orders ('though his poetic intention', sneered von Sternberg later, 'to suggest altering the sex of the devil was meant to aid in selling the picture, it did not do so'), it was said by its director to be a 'final tribute to the lady I had seen lean against the wings of a Berlin stage in 1929'. In it she was to play a turn-of-the-century Spanish charmer hotly pursued by Cesar Romero (in a rôle quit by Joel McCrea after 'differences' with von Sternberg) and Lionel Atwill through a plot in which, said the *Journal-American* later, 'the action is so absurd, so artificial, so repetitious that every scene fairly shrieks for Jim Cagney and a grapefruit'.

This nevertheless is the only picture of which Dietrich herself retains a print, and addicts maintain that it is a total summary of the romantic, elusive pictorial partnership she maintained across five years with von Sternberg—a marvellously moody, highly Satanic picture and ultimately as arch as the Admiralty. All this did not however do it much good at the box-office and its world release was not helped by a complaint from the Spanish government that it showed a civil guard drinking at a café and therefore insulted the honour of the Spanish armed forces.

During the shooting, von Sternberg suddenly announced that this would be his last film with Dietrich: 'She and I have progressed as far as possible together', he added, 'and my being with her will help neither

75-56

'A tedious hyperbole' (Time Magazine): *Dietrich as* The Scarlet Empress *(1934)*

Dietrich and Shirley Temple, co-starring only for the photograph. Miss Temple's first screen kiss was however received while she was playing 'Morelegs Sweetrick' in a parody of Dietrich and 'Morocco'

her nor me.' Dietrich has always maintained that she was both shocked and saddened by the decision; 'I didn't leave von Sternberg. He left me. That's very important. In my life, he was the man I wanted to please most. But he decided not to work with me any more. I was not happy about that. Perhaps I'm wrong, though, to suggest I was deeply unhappy about it either: you can't be made really unhappy by something you're not interested in, and my heart was never in that work. I had no desire to be a film actress, to always play somebody else, to be always beautiful with somebody constantly straightening out your eyelashes.'

Yet despite the studio's shoddy treament of von Sternberg, and despite her own avowed distaste for the life of a film star, Dietrich at this time made no very determined effort to interrupt her contractual arrangements with Paramount—though in all fairness it should perhaps be added that, having settled herself and her family firmly in California, she had little choice. The box-office failure of her last two films cannot have made her freelance prospects look unduly rosy. But her relationship with von Sternberg had in any case always been as hazy as her relationship with Rudolf Sieber: asked about the 'Svengali' legend she replied, 'We gave that to the press so they would leave us alone', and in the end it seems she was content to be thrown back on her own resources within the studio framework.

For many film-goers, C. H. Rand among them, the screen image of Marlene Dietrich now transcended its creators:

I would cheerfully walk ten miles to see a film that had Marlene Dietrich in it, or motor five hundred miles through snow. I know well enough, of course, that the enchantment is not Marlene alone. I see her through the eyes of cunning artists. I see her through the eyes of Josef von Sternberg. I see her through the eyes of her talented cameramen, art directors and dress designers. I see her in shot after shot of almost too perfect composition until she moves in a world of her own ... Like all the great film characters, Marlene is a myth, a symbol, an idea. And it is because she is the perfect embodiment of that idea that she had this fascination for me ... I find all my

requisites in the screen character of Marlene Dietrich. She has beauty in abundance. She has a rich, sensual allure. And you have only to look at her eyes to see that she has brains, and at her mouth to see that she has humour.

Significantly, it was the legend of a much later age who starred in the 1960 remake of *The Devil Is A Woman* . . . Brigitte Bardot.

But with von Sternberg finished at Paramount, Dietrich's career was left in the hands of Ernst Lubitsch who promptly put her into *Desire* with Gary Cooper and John Halliday under the direction of Frank Borzage. An elegant light comedy which did no one lasting harm and Paramount's accountants a little good, it moved Dietrich subtly but firmly back into 'acceptable' mainstream stardom and away from the more intriguing if risky bisexuality of her von Sternberg image.

Yet she remained above and beyond Hollywood: perhaps the only one of its great thirties stars never to get an Oscar, she was also distanced from the movie establishment of the time, leading a highly private life in which her name was linked at different times to everyone from Maurice Chevalier and David Niven to (more plausibly) John Gilbert

A couple of Hollywood broads: Dietrich at a party with her hostess, the Countess di Frasso, 1935

'*The best production of the Dietrich/Sternberg alliance since* Blue Angel' (New York Times): The Devil Is A Woman *(1935)*

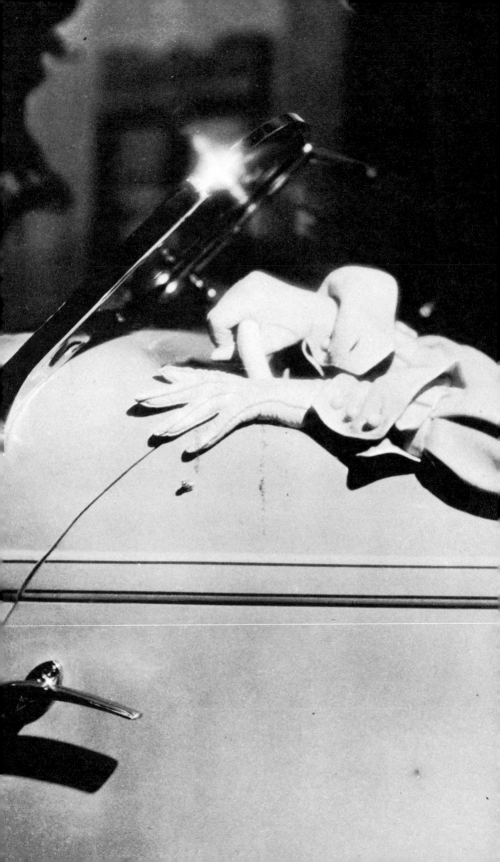

PREVIOUS PAGE
The jewel thief in Borzage's Desire *(1936)*

Dietrich and Gary Cooper on the set of Desire *watched by (left to right) Robert Pittack the assistant cameraman, Charles Lang the director of photography and Frank Borzage the director*

and Erich Maria Remarque and Douglas Fairbanks Jr., Niven retains fond memories of her at this time:

> She had a black Cadillac driven by a chauffeur named Briggs who carried two revolvers and in winter wore a uniform with mink collar ... once I was ill with flu in my chalet shack on North Vista Street: she hardly knew me but Briggs was a friend and he told her I was sick. Marlene arrived with soup and medicine. She then went to work and herself cleaned the whole place up from top to bottom, changed my bedclothes and departed. She came back every day until I was well.

Professionally, however, things were going from bad to worse; after the so-so success of *Desire* Paramount put her into *I Loved A Soldier*, a Henry Hathaway remake of an old Pola Negri vehicle in which Dietrich's co-star was Charles Boyer. Far from being the romantic, charm-laden picture which might have been anticipated, the film aborted when Dietrich quarrelled with its producer over the John van Druten script and walked off the set after twenty-eight days' shooting. Paramount, having already spent $900,000, borrowed Margaret Sullavan from Universal to complete: she however tripped over a light cable and broke an arm, by which time the budget was up to a million. When the picture finally appeared as *Hotel Imperial* in 1939, its stars were Ray Milland and Isa Miranda.

Dietrich promptly sailed for London, where she made a deal with her old UFA director Alexander Korda to film *Knight Without Armour*. While he was setting up the rest of the cast she returned to Hollywood where Paramount loaned her to David O. Selznick (the producer who had once remarked that Sternberg 'made Dietrich up out of rolls of old cloth, admittedly star-spangled') for a Boyer–Basil Rathbone opus called *The Garden of Allah*. Some indication of her current standing in Hollywood can however be gleaned from a letter sent by Selznick to Dietrich's friend Gregory Ratoff while he was negotiating her contract:

> As far as Marlene goes, I am very pleased that she is interested in joining me ... but you will have to get over to her some facts which I

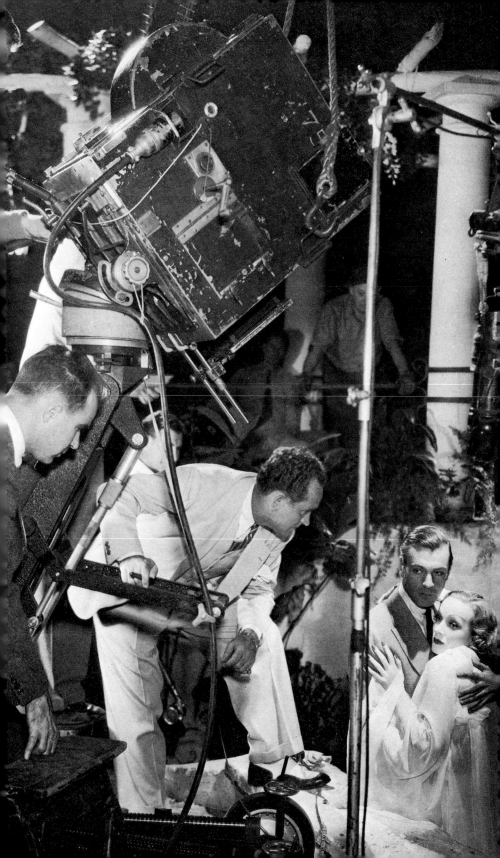

Briggs, the limousine and the life of a Hollywood star in the late 1930s

doubt she at present appreciates. Any sales manager or important theatre man will tell you—or indeed will tell her, if he is honest—that she has been hurt to such a terrible extent that she is no longer even a fairly important box-office star. There is no personality so important that he or she can survive the perfectly dreadful line-up of pictures that Marlene has had. . . . She is in no position to command any fabulous salary . . . I am perfectly willing to give her a percentage deal whereby, if she thinks she is bigger than I think she is at the moment, she will get what perhaps she thinks she is entitled to; and whereby, further, she will get all the money she can possibly want if, and when, she again becomes the star that she was after *Morocco* and before the long line-up of *Dishonored*, *Song Of Songs*, *The Blonde Venus*, *The Scarlet Empress* etc. . . . I frankly want her on the right terms; I think she is one of the most magnificent personalities that the screen has had in many years and I think it is a crying shame that she had been dragged down as she has been. . . .

In the end Dietrich was paid $200,000 for *The Garden of Allah* (a fair reward, perhaps, for having to stand there straightfaced while a bit-player told her 'Go to the Desert . . . and in the face of the infinite your grief will lessen') and of the film itself Graham Greene was later to write a review which I reprint here in its entirety from the *Spectator* of 25 December 1936, if only because it seems to me such a perfect summary of the proceedings:

Mr Charles Boyer, a runaway monk from a Trappist monastery in North Africa, and Miss Marlene Dietrich, a lovely orphan heiress suffering from world weariness, meet in a Moroccan dance hall. A desert soothsayer does his best to warn the woman against her doom ('I see a camel by a church door, and then a tent in the far desert' as he describes it with Surrealist fervour) and so does the local Catholic priest, who distrusts this man who is apt to stagger uneasily back at the sight of a crucifix. 'This is the land of fire' he says, 'and you are a woman of fire.' Nobody talks less apocalyptically than that: the great abstractions come whistling hoarsely out in Miss Dietrich's stylized, weary and monotonous whisper, among the hideous Technicolour flowers, the yellow cratered desert like Gruyère cheese, the beige faces. Startling sunsets bloom behind silhouetted camels very much as in the gaudy little pictures which used to be on sale on the pavements of Trafalgar Square. Needless to say—but many thousands of feet are expended in saying it—the pair are married by the Catholic priest (according to the Church of England service) and there, waiting for them outside the church door, is The Camel, the foredoomed camel, ready to carry them, with an escort of twenty-five armed Arabs, on their honeymoon—to that Tent in the Far Desert. There fate has a coincidence in store for them in the person of a French officer lost in the Sahara with his men. 'We are a

*'Go to the Desert . . . and in the
face of the Infinite your grief will
lessen.'* (The Garden of Allah,
1936)

Filming Charles Boyer on
The Garden of Allah *location*

'For taking two baths, revealing her beautiful legs and shedding a hollow-cheeked glamour through 9,000 feet of British film she got $450,000. This makes her, on a job basis, the highest paid woman in the world.' (Life) Knight Without Armour *(1937)*

'As hauntingly beautiful as ever' (Herald-Tribune): *Dietrich in* Angel *(1937)*

lost patrol' he succinctly explains to the lady in a low-backed evening dress who is waving a lighted torch from the top of a ruined tower (the Surrealism of this film is really magnificent). He recognises the former monk (he had been a guest in the monastery) and sitting together on the Gruyère cheese, silhouetted like camels, the lovers make the great decision to renounce all. The Catholic priest (Mr Aubrey Smith, who has kept a straight county bat to the bodyline bowling) shakes hands all round at the railway station, the monk slowly wends his way up an avenue of cypresses, a grey glove flaps from the window of four-wheeler. Alas! my poor Church, so picturesque, so noble, so superhumanly pious, so intensely dramatic. I really prefer the *New Statesman* view, shabby priests counting pesetas on their fingers in dingy cafés before blessing tanks. Even the liqueur made at this Trappist monastery is Mysterious. Only one monk at a time knows the secret of its making, and when Mr Charles Boyer disappears from the monastery the secret is irrecoverably lost. The thought that this sweet and potent drink will be once again obtainable during licensed hours mitigates for us the agony of the parting.

Undaunted by that or apparently any other review, Dietrich followed *The Garden of Allah* with *Knight Without Armour* for which she got $450,000 and co-star billing with Robert Donat who, already suffering from the asthma which blighted his career, seemed at times unlikely to be able to complete the picture, an inability which gave rise to rumours that Laurence Olivier would be taking over as the valiant Englishman caught up in the Russian revolution (a plot which indicated, wrote one critic later, that it was ghastly to be a White Russian, equally ghastly to be a Red Russian, but infinitely preferable to be English at all times). Dietrich however refused to work with anyone else, and Donat completed the picture—one which has stood the test of time rather better than much of Dietrich's other work in the thirties, due perhaps to a distinguished supporting cast (Irene Vanbrugh, John Clements, Herbert Lomas, Austin Trevor) and some superb camerawork from Harry Stradling and a young Jack Cardiff.

They too were more than a little impressed by Dietrich's technical knowledge, as Stradling remembers: 'While each shot was being lined up she had a full-length mirror set up beside the camera and was able to see just how she would look on the screen. If she thought the light on her arms was too strong, or her shoulders were catching too much from a certain arc, she never hesitated to say so; and she was always right.'

Even Graham Greene was more enthusiastic this time: he described *Knight Without Armour* as 'a first-class thriller' though of Dietrich he added: 'She never acts. She lends her too beautiful body: she consents to pose: she is the marble motive for heroisms and sacrifices: as for acting—that is merely the word for what goes on all round her: she leaves it to her servants.'

Dietrich's return to America was for another Lubitsch production (*Angel*) co-starring Herbert Marshall and Melvyn Douglas; it marked however the end of her long association with Paramount who seemed as depressed as any of the critics by the sheer, bland awfulness of it. 'The film comes to a full stop' wrote the *New York Times* 'every time she raises or lowers the artificially elongated Dietrich eyelids—and she hoists them up and down at one-minute intervals like the Strong Man handling a 1,000-pound weight in a sideshow.'

With Herbert Marshall and director/producer Ernst Lubitsch (right) on the set of Angel

Dietrich 1931–41: a decade of hats

Dietrich recreated: Destry Rides Again *(1939)*

7

Where have all the young men gone?
Gone to graveyards, every one.

DIETRICH'S HOLLYWOOD CAREER seemed over: 'she will be permitted to work elsewhere' announced Paramount tersely, though for almost two years she in fact failed to work at all. Various projects were mooted, including a film of Rattigan's *French Without Tears* (the first of a number of occasions on which it was suggested that Dietrich should film Rattigan, and though she never did one can see the reasoning—few actresses appear better equipped to portray his semi-detached heroines) but Paramount paid her a reputed $200,000 *not* to make the film after a list of 1937 star ratings placed her at number 126.

At the end of 1937, a group of independent film distributors had taken a red-bordered advertisement in the *Hollywood Reporter* listing those actors and actresses whom they considered to be 'box-office poison' and Dietrich's name featured high on it, admittedly in the distinguished company of Katharine Hepburn, Joan Crawford, Fred Astaire and Mae West. But her rescue from total screen oblivion did not come until the beginning of 1939, and then from an unlikely source.

Universal Pictures, which was then in severe financial trouble, had brought in three new executives trained in economics rather than artistry; their task was to see what could be done with existing (and therefore cheap) studio property. Among this property they happened upon the script for a 1932 Tom Mix western called *Destry Rides Again* which they assigned to Joe Pasternak for a remake; he promptly had it rewritten as a satire on all the other westerns he had ever seen and then some.

Failing to get his first choice (Paulette Goddard), Pasternak cast Dietrich—alongside James Stewart—as 'Frenchy', a wild western saloon-bar entertainer; he gave her songs by Frank Loesser and Friedrich (now Frederick) Hollander, the latter of whom had of course scored *The Blue Angel* and written 'Jonny', the song she sang in *Song of Songs* and which was to remain—with all the Hollander numbers—at the very heart of her post-war cabaret routines.

Understandably, Dietrich had her doubts about appearing in a comic western, and for a salary of only $50,000 at that; from high horse to horse opera seemed a formidable career leap even for a career in as

With George Raft in Manpower *(1941): 'As the clip-joint babe, Marlene Dietrich sings a husky song, crosses a pair of nifty legs, bakes a batch of biscuits and, as has become customary in recent successes, gets slapped around.'* (Life)

Smoke gets in your eyes—from Manpower

much trouble as hers. Not for the first time she turned to von Sternberg for advice, and not for the first time he put her right: 'What Pasternak has in mind will be very effective. I put you on a pedestal, the untouchable goddess. He wants to drag you down into the mud, very touchable—a bona fide goddess with feet of clay. Very good salesmanship.'

Dietrich took his advice, played the part, and the result was a reverse-casting triumph which allowed her to end the 1930s the way she had begun them: in a screen triumph. She was by now in severe tax troubles ($142,000 claimed, though with her customary persistence she counter-sued the taxmen and ended up some years later with a refund) but at least it looked as though her career was set fair again: *Destry* (and in particular the fist-fight with Una Merkel) had given her a new lease of life in films, although without a new Sternberg-figure it was to prove an oddly restricting and ultimately disappointing one. In three of her next four films (*Seven Sinners, Manpower, The Spoilers*) she was stereotyped as a bar-room singer.

A picture of her at the time of *Manpower* in 1941 comes from her co-star, Edward G. Robinson:

My first impression of Miss Dietrich made me nervous because, to carp, she appeared to have such arrogant self-assurance and security. I had never met her before, though I had seen all her pictures and was aware that she was sexy, temperamental, demanding, beautiful, and perhaps the synthetic creation of Josef von Sternberg.

Playing with her, I learned that we shared a common passion: work. More than that: Be on time, know the lines, toe the marks, say the words, be ready for anything. God, she was beautiful—and still is—but I don't think it interested her very much. Beauty, that obsessive sexual thing she had, and her superficial self-confidence were simply instruments to help her bank account and her art.

One of the things about here that astonished me most was her knowledge of the technical side of motion pictures. She seemed to know everything. She constantly watched the camera and the

With John Wayne and Harry Carey in The Spoilers *(1942)*

Paramount's legendary sirens: Mae West visits Dietrich and Raoul Walsh on the Manpower *set*

lighting, and she would politely superintend, make suggestions to the cameramen and gaffers so subtly and so sexily that no one was offended, and she got precisely what she wanted. . . . My view of her as an actress? I am not sure I would call it talent; it is something beyond that—mystery, unavailability, distance, feminine mystique (before those two words got to mean something else). I gladly risk the sneer of Germaine Greer: I like the Dietrich mystique better than the Greer. Certainly, while Betty Friedan may be more intelligent, I'd rather spend my time with Marlene who, by the way, is one of the best gourmet and family cooks about and certainly should and could be called Ms. Kleen. She is the quintessential sex goddess: she is also the quintessential German hausfrau. She is mother as sex; sex as it was intended. She is rough and tough—and absolutely uniquely and gloriously herself.

During the war, Dietrich also starred in René Clair's first American film *The Flame of New Orleans*, and consented to be sawn in half by Orson Welles for an all-star package called *Follow the Boys*. Other and still less remarkable work included *The Lady Is Willing* and *Pittsburgh* (both 1942) and *Kismet* (1944) but by now there was every indication that her heart was no longer exclusively—if indeed it had ever been—in the film business. With Sieber and Maria settled in California (Sieber having abandoned the movie business for a chicken farm in the San Fernando valley, where he was to live contentedly for the next thirty years) and her sister Elisabeth in a German concentration camp Dietrich herself was torn between America, where she knew she could get films however terrible the scripts might be, and Europe where she felt she wanted to be involved in some as yet unspecified war work. An American citizen since 1939, she volunteered for USO—the American Entertainments organisation—and in 1943 found herself in North Africa at the start of what was effectively to become a three-year series of troop concerts.

Her celebrated introduction to 'Lili Marlene', an introduction she was still using in concert as late as the summer of 1975, gives some indication of her wartime travels:

Now here's a song that is very close to my heart: I sang it during the war. I sang it for three long years: all through Africa, Sicily,

Swearing American citizenship, 9 June 1939. The German press announced 'Frequent contact with Jews renders her entirely un-German'

Italy; through Alaska, Greenland, Iceland; through England, through France, through Belgium and Holland, through Germany and into Czechoslovakia.

Her war work, she said later, was the only important thing she had ever done and in the U.S. it won her a 'Champion War Bond Salesman of the Nation' award as well as the affection of countless servicemen. Four months after the invasion she was in Germany with Patton's army, entertaining, lecturing in Army study centres, visiting hospitals and generally doing whatever she was asked. After it was all over, and her sister was freed from Belsen, the French made Dietrich a Chevalière of the Legion of Honour and the Americans gave her the Congress Medal of Freedom; but in more selfish terms those wartime tours were to prove immensely valuable to Dietrich herself. On them she learnt (in much the same way and at much the same time as her old friend Noël Coward was learning) that away from all the trappings of a production unit she could work entirely alone, aided perhaps by a piano and a good lighting man, but essentially answerable to nobody but herself and her audience. It was the beginning of Dietrich as a solo entertainer, a development she owes very largely to an American comedian called Danny Thomas:

I was appearing with him in troop concerts in Italy in 1944, and he taught me everything—how to deal with an audience, how to answer if they shout, how to play them, how to make them laugh. Above all, he taught me to talk to them. I used to do some conjuring tricks Orson Welles had shown me; we were working off the back of a lorry and one night some soldiers began to jeer and interrupt. Somehow I dealt with them and Danny said 'That's it—that's all I have to teach you.' Soon after that he left me to go back to America and I was on my own in the concerts and that's how it's been ever since. Once you have caught the attention of front-line troops who may be about to die tomorrow and know it, then you can catch the attention of anybody anywhere. Nothing else in my life has ever been quite so difficult—or quite so rewarding.

Dietrich's success in her troop concerts cannot be overestimated; blessed with the huskiest voice and the best legs in the business, but more than a little hindered by the fact that (as David Niven recalls) a large number of her audiences took it for granted that with a name like that she had to be some kind of German spy, she put together an act involving little more than herself and (for a while) a bizarre kind of musical saw which she would play on request. But it was the songs which carried her through: deep-throated, husky, mannish laments for lost loves, lost youth, lost ideals, they seemed to summarise a post-battle mood which mingled relief at still being alive with uncertainty about whether life itself had been worth all the fighting for.

War: Dietrich on board the Korbin with Jean Gabin (far right) and the French Navy

War: Dietrich arrives in London, 1944, in USO uniform

War: Dietrich in Germany with a contingent of GIs

Dietrich and Irving Berlin on the war-bond trail
With Maria, also now in uniform, at El Morocco in New York
Dietrich and her mother, together again, 1945
The million-dollar legs: Dietrich's post-war return to the U.S.

Dietrich was not, evidently, a 'war entertainer' in the mindlessly British patriotic idiom of a Vera Lynn: her songs were not about a single country or a single victory or a single affair, but rather about the survival of mankind itself, and to that extent she sang not so much for the Allies as for Europe—a prolonged marching song, part cynical, part romantic, for and about a continent which had just torn itself apart yet again. It was the beginning of Mother Courage.

It was also, of course, the beginning of her greatest song success: the American Office of Strategic Services decided, as part of its propaganda exercises, to have Dietrich record 'Lili Marlene' in English and at the same time a large number of American classics ('Miss Otis Regrets', 'Surrey With The Fringe On Top', 'Time On My Hands') in German. The latter recordings disappeared for several years into OSS files but 'Lili Marlene' became her standard, a song she was to use in almost every cabaret appearance from then onwards.

But for a while Dietrich was to return to her screen career: immediately after the war, in France with Jean Gabin (to whom her name was now plausibly being linked by an eager press) there was a plan that they should do *Les Portes de la Nuit* for Marcel Carne; not liking the script, however, Dietrich withdrew and Gabin with her. Instead they did the best-forgotten *Martin Roumagnac* after which Dietrich returned to Hollywood for a horror called *Golden Earrings* before re-establishing her screen credibility in 1948 with Billy Wilder's *A Foreign Affair* for which she played, unsurprisingly, a German nightclub singer. Then came a walk-on in *Jigsaw* and an also-starring rôle in *Stage Fright* (1950) for Alfred Hitchcock who noted somewhat acidly: 'Miss Dietrich is a professional—a professional actress, a professional dress designer, a professional cameraman', though in all fairness one might note that his film is only remarkable now for the one sequence in which Dietrich sings 'The Laziest Gal In Town', the Cole Porter song which she was later to add to her already considerable cabaret collection.

By now her daughter Maria, after her second marriage to a toy and set designer called William Riva (the first had been to a fellow-student at the University of Wisconsin) had the first of their four sons and

Dietrich was being tagged 'the world's most glamorous grandmother', an accolade she took—as all others—in her icy stride. Maria herself had become a familiar face on American television where she starred in countless live dramas during the early fifties while her mother pressed on to another 'guest star' job with her old Destry partner James Stewart—this one an uninspired British aviation thriller called *No Highway*. Then, again in Hollywood, she did Fritz Lang's *Rancho Notorious* playing inevitably a saloon bar singer in what was at best a very poor man's *Destry*.

'It was conceived for Marlene' Lang revealed some years later, 'but she resented going gracefully into a little tiny bit older category; she became younger and younger until finally it was hopeless . . . she was still very much under the influence of von Sternberg. She would say "Oh look, Sternberg would have done so and so." "Well" I said "but I am Lang" . . . it was very, very disagreeable. Maybe I was vain in thinking I could do something for her; maybe if she would have had trust in me . . . by the end of the picture we didn't speak to each other any more.'

After *Rancho Notorious* came a memorable moment in *Around the World in 80 Days* (a dance-hall queen in San Francisco, what else?) followed by a Vittorio de Sica disaster called *The Monte Carlo Story*. By now (1957) Dietrich had only three films left to make, if one is prepared—as many were—to overlook a walk-on in *Paris When It Sizzles*. Happily, each of them was to be a considerable improvement on anything else she had done since the war, and together they add up to a not undignified conclusion to a screen career which had had, to say the least, its ups and downs.

With Gabin at the time of Martin Roumagnac *(1946)*

With Maria, now herself an actress, at Judy Garland's Palace opening, October 1951

'*The heartless siren who lures men to degradation and goes on singing*': *in Billy Wilder's* A Foreign Affair *(1948) with Hollander at the piano*

With James Stewart and Glynis Johns in No Highway *(1951)*

Promoting Around The World *with (in foreground) Buster Keaton, Joe E. Brown, Cantinflas, Shirley MacLaine and David Niven*

With Shirley MacLaine, George Raft, David Niven: Around The World in 80 Days *(1956)*

Christine Vole on the stand: Witness For The Prosecution *(1958)*

With Charles Laughton, Tyrone Power and Billy Wilder setting up Witness For The Prosecution *(1958)*

'Lay off the candy bars': *Dietrich and Welles in his* Touch of Evil *(1958)*

With Spencer Tracy (in dark glasses) on location for Kramer's Judgement at Nuremberg *(1961)*

First, in 1958, came *Witness For The Prosecution* which reunited her with Billy Wilder who drew from her a superb double-performance as Christine Vole, a favourite part, said Dietrich, 'because she's not only brave but she loves her man unconditionally. She's the kind of woman I like best.'

In the same year, disguised under a black wig belonging to Elizabeth Taylor and smoking a cigar, Dietrich did *Touch of Evil* for Orson Welles, nominally a guest star rôle but in fact by far the most memorable in a picture which also featured Welles himself, Charlton Heston, Janet Leigh and Akim Tamiroff to say nothing of other 'guest' appearances by Joseph Cotten, Zsa Zsa Gabor and Mercedes McCambridge. Dietrich played the brothel-keeper who has the laconic last words about Welles—'he was some kind of a man . . . but what does it matter what you say about people?' and with them created a screen memory only supplanted by her last appearance to date (1975), in Stanley Kramer's 1961 *Judgement at Nuremberg:* 'What did he know' she asks of her dead husband, a Nazi General, 'about the crimes they tried him for . . . he became part of the revenge which the victors always take upon the vanquished.'

And that, apart from the narration for a Second World War documentary called *The Black Fox* which won an Academy Award in 1962, is the sum total of Dietrich's screen work: 'a few cans of celluloid on the junkheap someday' as her character in *No Highway* had remarked, though it's possible some of the cans will prove hard to burn.

Dietrich, one suspects, is not going to care much one way or the other: on 15 December 1953 she had started a whole new career as a cabaret entertainer at the Hotel Sahara in Las Vegas, and within six months she was at the Café de Paris in London, 'the legendary, lovely Marlene' of Coward's introduction to her quoted at the beginning this book.

Dietrich at Las Vegas, 1959

*Coming Attraction
Theatre De' Etoile*

8

Love's always been my game
Play it how I may
I was born that way
I just can't help it . . .

DIETRICH IN CABARET, leaving no rhines-
tone unturned, is something else: picking up an average of $30,000 a
week and playing virtually wherever and whenever she chose, she had
at long last discovered a job she truly enjoyed doing so much that she
had no qualms about turning down both *Pal Joey* and *Gigi* in favour of
cabaret seasons around the world. To suggest that her cabaret success
gave Dietrich a new lease of life is to put it mildly; twenty years after
that Las Vegas opening, Peter Bogdanovich found himself sitting
behind a now seventy-three-year-old lady on a plane to Denver: 'Why
am I going to sing in Denver? Because I'm an optimist, that's why.'
Seeing her concert there, Bogdanovich noticed:

> She also transcends her material. Whether it's a flighty old tune
> like 'I Can't Give You Anything But Love, Baby' or 'My Blue
> Heaven', a schmaltzy German love song, 'Das Lied ist Aus', or a
> French one 'La Vie en Rose', she lends each an air of the aristocrat,
> yet she never patronises. She transforms Charles Trenet's 'I Wish
> You Love' by calling it 'a love song sung to a child' and then singing
> it that way. No one else can now sing Cole Porter's 'The Laziest Gal
> In Town'—it belongs to her. As much as 'Lola' and 'Falling in Love
> Again' always have. She kids 'The Boys in the Back Room' from
> *Destry Rides Again* but with great charm. Singing in German, 'Jonny'
> becomes frankly erotic. A folk song, 'Go 'Way From My Window' has
> never been done with such passion, and in her hands 'Where Have All
> The Flowers Gone?' is not just another anti-war lament but a tragic
> accusation against us all. Another pacifist song, written by an
> Australian, has in it a recurring lyric—'The war is over—seems we
> won' and each time she sings it a deeper nuance is revealed.

But what Bogdanovich was seeing for the first time was an act which
had been carefully nailed together across innumerable performances
in countless countries: backed as often as not by a thirty-piece
orchestra, lit by Joe Davis and sustained throughout by the super-
lative orchestrations of Burt Bacharach (of whom she once said 'he is
my teacher, my critic, my accompanist, my conductor and my

arranger. I wish I could also say he is my composer but that isn't true: he is everyone's composer'), she and her act had already drawn paeans of almost embarrassing praise from such widely diverse observers as Jean Cocteau, Ernest Hemingway and Kenneth Tynan.

By now, by 1975, Bacharach's arrangements seem to have survived a decade and Dietrich herself seems to have survived a century. At the end of each and every one of her performances there is a standing ovation, somehow it never quite seems enough.

When she went back to Germany, in 1959, there were ugly rumours that her opposition to the Nazi regime had made her enemies who even now would not hesitate to make their presence felt at her opening: in fact, however, the Berlin concert was a major triumph even by Dietrich's post-war cabaret standards: 'from the first bar of her first song' wrote the Berlin *Tagesiegel* next day 'there was jubilation in the hall for this reunion with a woman who has about her the aura of Berlin ... a reunion with a sound that was more than the effect of her singing. It was the sound of an epoch.'

But what of the woman herself? Dividing her time between Paris, New York and California, spending more of it with her husband and grandchildren as the years passed, she remained a curiously elusive figure, fleetingly glimpsed at airports or press conferences called to launch yet another concert. Art Buchwald claims he got closer to the real Dietrich:

When one thinks of Marlene Dietrich [he wrote in 1956] one conjures up the vision of a beautiful glamour girl who has held on to the title, long after others have fallen by the wayside, so to speak. You think of her as a cool, exquisitely dressed lady who has given every woman over thirty-five hope for the future, and has even made the word 'grandmother' sound sexy.

But there is another side to Miss Dietrich that only her friends know about. To them she is a modern Florence Nightingale, whose most important purpose in life is to bring comfort to the sick and encouragement to the wounded, and cook chicken-noodle soup for the depressed. There has probably been no one in show business who has been so concerned about the health and welfare of her friends than Miss Dietrich.

In 1972, Dietrich picked up just over £100,000 for a controversial TV special about which neither she nor her producer Alexander Cohen seemed any too happy; Rex Reed asked her why she was still at work? 'What am I supposed to do, stay home and knit? Besides, I need the money, honey. Nobody believes me when I tell them I am poor: American taxes bleed me dry. I have to support my daughter Maria and four grandchildren. The money I made from this show will keep them going for years. . . .'

A few months later she expanded on the theme to Clive Hirschhorn:

This is the economy-class seat in the BOAC VC 10. Part of a great aircraft. The VC10 gets off the ground faster. Lands sooner. With its Rolls-Royce engines, it's the most powerful, the most advanced airliner in the world. The VC10 is triumphantly sure, silent, serene. Swift because of the powerful engines. Silent because these engines are at the back, so all the noise gets left behind. Serene because each seat is a miracle in design. A leg-stretching, back-resting armchair of a seat. And flying in the BOAC VC10 costs no more than ordinary aircraft.

ALL OVER THE WORLD BOAC TAKES GOOD CARE OF YOU ✈ **BOAC VC10**

BRITISH OVERSEAS AIRWAYS CORPORATION

*With her conductor Burt Bacharach (left) and her lighting expert Joe
Davis arriving at Edinburgh airport for the 1964 Festival*

Do you think this is glamorous? That it's a great life and that I do
it for my health? Well it isn't. Maybe once, but not now ... it's
because I pay away in taxes 88 cents out of each dollar I earn. Besides,
everybody in America works today. Oh, I know, I could be tucked
away out of sight in some Swiss chalet—but why should I? I am an
American citizen and proud to be so. I enjoy living in that country
and one pays for one's pleasures. So I work. People say that I have
some sort of quality—well, maybe I have. How am I to know that? All
I know is that I walk on to a stage, stand still, and sing. I think it is
Dietrich the woman they come to see, rather than Dietrich the
singer. They pay to see me for what I am. Particularly the English
audiences ... they like me because I do not take myself too
seriously.

In June 1973 Dietrich was in Britain doing a month-long provincial
tour and I went to see her and the act in Cardiff: neither had much
changed since I'd first encountered them a decade earlier—'Lola' was
still there, and 'Lili Marlene', and 'The Boys in the Back Room' and 'La
Vie en Rose' and all the other songs which tell you, in Tynan's
memorable phrase, that whatever hell you happen to inhabit she has
been there first and survived.

Going backstage afterwards, I encountered roughly five hundred
soberly dressed Welshmen and their wives already waiting at the stage
door for the privilege of scrambling over each other a few minutes later
in the surge to get her autograph. And what they got, some on
programmes, others on scraps of paper, others still on handbags was
quite simply 'Dietrich'. No 'Marlene', no 'Love', no 'Best Wishes'; just
the surname, written boldly and patiently with that same splendid
isolation which has always characterised her on the stage. Dietrich
does not ask for sympathy, or love, or pity—she asks merely for our
attention which is precisely what she gets.

Back at the hotel, I asked her why she thought they still turned out
to see her in such numbers?

Who knows? They certainly don't come to see me just because I take all the trouble to look as good as I can. In Russia once they said it was because I represented something—courage, stamina, faith, motherhood, who knows? Laurence Olivier once asked me 'How can you go out there every night all alone—no Shakespeare, no other actors, nothing?' But it's because I go out alone that I can be myself, and when they applaud they're applauding maybe what I've done, maybe what I've tried to stand for, or maybe just what they hope I'm going to deliver. Some nights of course they just sit there in stunned silence, amazed that I'm still alive and moving at all.

Piaf, Chevalier, Garland, Coward . . . is Dietrich the last survivor of that particular line of solo entertainers?

No, there's still Sinatra, Streisand, Minnelli. Now she, Liza, she's the only one I still stand in the wings to watch. She'll do what we've done, maybe more; you see she enjoys it, and that's the secret. Whenever I see people shivering before a show with stage fright I tell them to go do something else—there are other professions to choose, God knows. If you're taking money off an audience, you have no right to insecurity; if I'd ever been nervous I'd have done something else, made hats maybe. I make good hats.

Mobbed, even in Argentina

*Dietrich
on Broadway, 1967*

Thirty years after The Blue Angel, *Dietrich and Sternberg meet again in Berlin*

Sad? Sure I'm sad sometimes, when I think of the people I've lost: Hemingway, Cocteau, Remarque, Coward. My life today would be pretty empty without my daughter and grandsons—children give you a reason to go on living. There's always the chance they may need you. Without them you might as well go jump in the lake.

But privately, you know, I've never been able to take my life too seriously. Ever since I lost my country and my language, ever since I left Germany in 1930, I've been a traveller without many roots and if that's what you are then there isn't the time, thank God, to start examining yourself too closely. People seem to want to see me, though, and I guess for as long as they do I'll stay around.

Age has withered Dietrich, to the extent that in close-up she now looks about sixty, but custom has done little to stale a variety which

With the Beatles, Royal Command Performance, Prince of Wales's Theatre, London 1963

1964, Queen's Theatre, Shaftesbury Avenue: 'Look me over closely, tell me what you see . . .'

she herself would admit has been something less than infinite; the fact that her repertoire has not changed, and that she has not altered a single word of the autobiographical murmurings which link her songs in the ten years since I first saw her act, is merely proof of her theory that once you've got something right you may as well leave it that way. Her curtain call, like everything else about her, is a work of art and when she finally disappears from the stage, still wearing the kind of clothes that royalty ought to wear and somehow never do, it is the last great conjuring trick, executed with all the steely precision of the earlier ones. Imperturbable and unclassifiable, like a traveller in some exotic time-machine, Dietrich seems to bear no relation to her surroundings and, indeed, to have little idea of where geographically she is; artistically she has little doubt that it's home. To evoke nostalgia and then transcend it has perhaps been her greatest gift, that and a healthy sense of what in the theatre constitutes value for money: 'in real life most film people are a disappointment. I, on the other hand, am better in real life than on the movies.'

1964: Variety Theatre, Moscow: 'I just can't help it'

Grandmarlene, London 1975

'Look me over closely, tell me what you see': what one sees now is a formidable old German lady in a remarkable state of repair. But even she, as she is reluctantly beginning to concede, cannot last forever; as for me, I shall tell my children and probably my grandchildren that I saw Dietrich work. They may not care, but I do.

Dietrich at 75

Filmography

Der Kleine Napoleon (Union-Film, Berlin, 1923): George Jacoby (Director); Robert Liebmann, George Jacoby (Screenplay); with Egon von Hagen, Paul Heidemann, Loni Nest.

Die Tragödie Der Liebe (Joe May-Film, Berlin, 1923): Joe May (Director); Leo Birinski, Adolf Lantz (Screenplay); with Emil Jannings, Erika Glassner.

Der Mensch Am Wege (Osmania-Film, Berlin, 1923): Wilhelm Dieterle (Director and Scenarist); with Wilhelm Dieterle, Alexander Granach.

Der Sprung Ins Leben (Messter-Film, Berlin, 1924): Johannes. Guter (Director); Franz Schulz (Screenplay); with Xenia Desny, Walter Rilla.

Die Freudlose Gasse (Hirschal-Sofar-Film, Berlin, 1925): Georg Wilhelm Pabst (Director); Willi Hass (Screenplay); with Jaro Furth, Greta Garbo, Karl Ettlinger, Countess Tolstoi, Werner Krauss.

Manon Lescaut (UFA-Film, Berlin, 1926): Arthur Robison (Director); Hans Kyser, Arthur Robison (Screenplay); with Lya De Putti, Vladimir Gaidarov.

Eine Du Barry Von Heute (Felsom-Film, Berlin, 1926): Alexander Korda (Director); Robert Liebmann, Alexander Korda, Paul Reboux (Screenplay); with Maria Corda, Alfred Abel.

Madame Wünscht Keine Kinder (Fox-Europa-Film, Berlin, 1926): Alexander Korda (Director); Adolf Lantz, Bela Balazs (Screenplay); with Maria Corda, Harry Liedtke.

Kopf Hoch, Charly! (Richter-Film, Berlin, 1926): Willi Wolff (Director); Robert Liebmann, Willi Wolff (Screenplay); with Anton Pointner, Ellen Richter.

Der Juxbaron (Richter-Film, Berlin, 1927): Willi Wolff (Director); Robert Liebmann, Willi Wolff (Screenplay); with Reinhold Schunzel, Henry Bender, Julia Serder.

Sein Grösster Bluff (Nero-Film, Berlin, 1927): Harry Piel (Director): Henrik Galeen (Screenplay); with Harry Piel, Tony Tetzlaff, Lotte Lorring.

Café Electric (Sascha-Film, Vienna, 1927): Gustav Ucicky (Director); Jacques Bachrach (Screenplay); with Fritz Alberti, Anny Coty, Willi Forst.

Prinzessin Olala (Super-Film, Berlin, 1928): Robert Land (Director); Franz Schulz, Robert Land (Screenplay); with Hermann Böttcher, Walter Rilla, Carmen Boni.

Ich Küsse Ihre Hand, Madame (Super-Film, Berlin, 1929): Robert Land (Director and Scenarist); with Harry Liedtke, Pierre de Guingand.

Die Frau, Nach Der Man Sich Sehnt (Terra-Film, Berlin, 1929): Kurt Bernhardt (Director); Ladislas Vajda (Screenplay); with Fritz Kortner, Frida Richard.

Das Schiff Der Verlorenen Menschen (Glass-Wengeroff-Film, Berlin, 1929): Maurice Tourneur (Director and Scenarist); with Fritz Kortner, Gaston Modot, Fedor Chaliapin Jr, Robin Irvine.

Gefahren Der Brautzeit (Strauss-Film, Berlin, 1929): Fred Sauer (Director); Walter Wassermann, Walter Schlee (Screenplay); with Willi Forst, Lotte Lorring, Ernst Stahl-Nachbaur.

Der Blaue Engel (Pommer-UFA Film, Berlin, 1930); Josef von Sternberg (Director); Robert Liebmann, etc. (Screenplay); with Emil Jannings, Kurt Gerron, Rosa Valetti, Hans Albers.

Morocco (Paramount, U.S.A., 1930): Josef von Sternberg (Director); Jules Furthman (Screenplay); with Gary Cooper, Adolphe Menjou, Juliette Compton.

Dishonored (Paramount, U.S.A., 1931): Josef von Sternberg (Director); Daniel H. Rubin (Screenplay); with Victor McLaglen, Lew Cody, Warner Oland, Bill Powell.

Shanghai Express (Paramount, U.S.A., 1932): Josef von Sternberg (Director); Jules Furthman (Screenplay); with Clive Brook, Anna May Wong, Warner Oland, Eugene Pallette.

Blonde Venus (Paramount, U.S.A., 1932): Josef von Sternberg (Director); Jules Furthman, S. K. Lauren (Screenplay); with Herbert Marshall, Cary Grant, Dickie Moore, Sterling Holloway, Hattie McDaniel.

Song of Songs (Paramount, U.S.A., 1933): Rouben Mamoulian (Director); Leo Birinski, Samuel Hoffenstein (Screenplay); with Brian Aherne, Lionel Atwill, Alison Skipworth.

The Scarlet Empress (Paramount, U.S.A., 1934): Josef von Sternberg (Director); Manuel Komroff (Screenplay); with John Lodge, Sam Jaffe, Louise Dresser, Maria Sieber, C. Aubrey Smith, Gavin Gordon.

The Devil is a Woman (Paramount, U.S.A., 1935): Josef von Sternberg (Director); John Dos Passos, S. K. Winston (Screenplay); with Lionel Atwill, Cesar Romero, Edward Everett Horton.

Desire (Paramount, U.S.A., 1936): Frank Borzage (Director); Edwin Justus Mayer, Waldemar Young, Samuel Hoffenstein (Screenplay); with Gary Cooper, John Halliday, Ernest Cossart, Akim Tamiroff.

I Loved a Soldier (Paramount, U.S.A., uncompleted, 1936): Henry Hathaway (Director); John van Druten (Screenplay); with Charles Boyer, Akim Tamiroff, Paul Lukas.

The Garden of Allah (Selznick/United Artists, U.S.A., 1936): Richard Boleslawski (Director); W. P. Lipscomb, Lynn Riggs (Screenplay); with Charles Boyer, Basil Rathbone, C. Aubrey Smith, Tilly Losch, Joseph Schildkraut, John Carradine.

Knight Without Armour (London Films, U.K., 1937): Jacques Feyder (Director); Lajos Biros, Arthur Wimperis (Screenplay); with Robert Donat, Irene Vanburgh, Herbert Lomas, Austin Trevor, David Tree, John Clements, Miles Malleson, Raymond Huntley.

Angel (Paramount, U.S.A., 1937): Ernst Lubitsch (Director); Samson Raphaelson (Screenplay); with Herbert Marshall, Melvyn Douglas, Edward Everett Horton, Laura Hope Crews, Ernest Cossart.

Destry Rides Again (Universal, U.S.A., 1939): George Marshall (Director); Felix Jackson, Henry Meyers, Gertrude Purcell (Screenplay); with James Stewart, Charles Winninger, Mischa Auer, Brian Donlevy, Una Merkel.

Seven Sinners (Universal, U.S.A., 1940): Tay Garnett (Director); John Meehan, Harry Tugend (Screenplay); with John Wayne, Broderick Crawford, Mischa Auer, Albert Dekker, Oscar Homolka.

The Flame of New Orleans (Universal, U.S.A., 1941): René Clair (Director); Norman Krasna (Screenplay); with Bruce Cabot, Roland Young, Andy Devine, Melville Cooper, Laura Hope Crews, Franklin Pangborn.

Manpower (Warner/First National, U.S.A., 1941): Raoul Walsh (Director); Richard Macaulay, Jerry Wald (Screenplay); with Edward G. Robinson, George Raft, Eve Arden, Frank McHugh, Barton MacLane.

The Lady is Willing (Columbia, U.S.A., 1942): Mitchell Leisen (Director); James Edward Grant, Albert McCleery (Screenplay); with Fred MacMurray, Aline McMahon, Sterling Holloway.

The Spoilers (Universal, U.S.A., 1942): Ray Enright (Director); Rex Beach (Original story); with Randolph Scott, John Wayne, Richard Barthelmess, Margaret Lindsay.

Pittsburgh (Universal, U.S.A., 1942): Lewis Seiler (Director); Tom Reed, Kenneth Gamet (Screenplay); with Randolph Scott, John Wayne, Louise Allbritton, Thomas Gomez.

Follow The Boys (Universal, U.S.A., 1944): Eddie Sutherland (Director); Lou Breslow, Gertrude Purcell (Screenplay); with George Raft, Vera Zorina, Orson Welles, Jeannette MacDonald, Dinah Shore, Donald O'Connor, W. C. Fields, The Andrews Sisters, Sophie Tucker, Arthur Rubinstein, Lon Chaney Jr, Andy Devine.

Kismet (MGM, U.S.A., 1944): William Dieterle (Director); John Meehan (Screenplay); with Ronald Colman, Edward Arnold, Joy Ann Page, James Craig.

Martin Roumagnac (Alcina, France, 1946): Georges Lacombe (Director); Pierre Very (Screenplay); with Jean Gabin, Daniel Gelin, Margo Lion.

Golden Earrings (Paramount, U.S.A., 1947): Mitchell Leisen (Director); Abraham Polonsky, Frank Butler, Helen Deutsch (Screenplay); with Ray Milland, Mervyn Vye, Bruce Lester, Dennis Hoey.

A Foreign Affair (Paramount, U.S.A., 1948) Billy Wilder (Director); Charles Brackett, Richard L. Breen, Billy Wilder (Screenplay); with Jean Arthur, John Lund, Millard Mitchell, Frederick Hollander.

Jigsaw (United Artists, U.S.A., 1949): Fletcher Markle (Director); Vincent McConnor, Fletcher Markle (Screenplay); with Franchot Tone, Jean Wallace, Henry Fonda, John Garfield, Burgess Meredith.

Stage Fright (Warner, U.K., 1950): Alfred Hitchcock (Director); Whitfield Cook (Screenplay); with Jane Wyman, Richard Todd, Michael Wilding, Alistair Sim, Kay Walsh, Sybil Thorndike, Miles Malleson, Andre Morell.

No Highway (Fox, U.K., 1951): Henry Koster (Director); R. C. Sherriff, Alec Coppel, Oscar Millard (Screenplay); with James Stewart, Glynis Johns, Jack Hawkins, Ronald Squire, Janette Scott, Kenneth More, Dora Bryan.

Rancho Notorious (RKO/Radio, U.S.A., 1952): Fritz Lang (Director); Daniel Tardash (Screenplay); with Arthur Kennedy, Mel Ferrer, Gloria Henry.

Around The World In 80 Days (Todd/United Artists, U.S.A., 1956): Michael Anderson (Director); S. J. Perelman, James Poe, John Farrow (Screenplay); with David Niven, Cantinflas, Shirley MacLaine, Robert Newton etc.

The Monte Carlo Story (United Artists/Titanus, Italy, 1957): Samuel Taylor (Director and Scenarist); with Vittorio de Sica, Arthur O'Connell, Natalie Trundy, Renato Rascel.

Witness For The Prosecution (United Artists, U.K., 1958): Billy Wilder (Director); Harry Kurnitz, Larry Marcus, Billy Wilder (Screenplay); with Tyrone Power, Charles Laughton, Elsa Lanchester, John Williams, Henry Daniell.

Touch Of Evil (Universal, U.S.A., 1958): Orson Welles (Director and Scenarist); with Charlton Heston, Janet Leigh, Orson Welles, Akim Tamiroff, Dennis Weaver, Zsa Zsa Gabor, Mercedes McCambridge, Joseph Cotten.

Judgement At Nuremburg (United Artists, U.S.A., 1961): Stanley Kramer (Director); Abby Mann (Screenplay); with Spencer Tracy, Burt Lancaster, Richard Widmark, Maximilian Schell, Judy Garland, Montgomery Clift, William Shatner, Werner Klemperer.

Black Fox (Heritage Films, U.K., 1962): Louis Clyde Stoumen (Director and Scriptwriter); Marlene Dietrich (Narrator).

Paris When It Sizzles (Paramount, France, 1964): Richard Quine (Director); George Axelrod (Screenplay); with William Hoden, Audrey Hepburn. Noël Coward, Tony Curtis, Mel Ferrer.

Radio
Throughout the late 1930s Marlene Dietrich did American radio broadcasts of many of her film scripts as well as those of others—she did *Grand Hotel* and *The Letter* (opposite Walter Pidgeon) for Lux Radio Theatre. Then in 1948 she was the hostess for a series of *General Electric Theater* and in 1952 she had an ABC series called *Café Istanbul*, thirty-minute adventure stories many of which she herself wrote. In 1964 she also starred in a BBC radio drama called *The Child*.

Television
One 'Special' for Alexander Cohen, ABC/BBC TV, 1972.

Recordings
Innumerable singles and LPs in English, German and French, of which perhaps the two most representative of her cabaret act are the albums 'Marlene Dietrich at the Café de Paris' (1954, introduction by Noël Coward), reissued 1975 on Hallmark SHM 834; and 'Dietrich in London' (1964) on Reprise CYP 169.

Bibliography

To all of the following authors, editors and publishers, British or American, living or defunct, I am most grateful for providing either direct quotations used (and acknowledged) in the text or else indirect background and reference material.

Agate, James, *Around Cinemas* (Second Series), Home & Van Thal, 1948
Baxter, John, *The Cinema of Josef von Sternberg*, Zwemmer; Barnes, 1971
Baxter, John, *Hollywood in the Thirties*, Zwemmer; Barnes, 1968
Behlmer, Rudy, *Memo from David O. Selznick*, Macmillan, 1973
Bogdanovich, Peter, *Fritz Lang in America*, Studio Vista, 1967
Bogdanovich, Peter, *Picture Shows*, Allen & Unwin, 1975
Brownlow, Kevin, *The Parade's Gone By*, Secker & Warburg, 1968
Bucher, Felix, *Germany* (Screen Series), Zwemmer; Barnes, 1970
Carr, Larry, *Four Fabulous Faces*, Arlington House, 1970
Cooke, Alistair (ed.), *Garbo and the Nightwatchmen*, Secker & Warburg, 1971
Crowther, Bosley, *The Great Films*, Putnam, 1967
Deschner, Donald, *The Films of Cary Grant*, Citadel, 1974
Dickens, Homer, *The Films of Gary Cooper*, Citadel, 1970
Dickens, Homer, *The Films of Marlene Dietrich*, Citadel, 1968
Dietrich, Marlene, *Marlene Dietrich's ABC*, Doubleday, 1962
Eisner, Lotte H., *The Haunted Screen*, Thames & Hudson, 1969
Fisher, John, *Call Them Irreplaceable*, Elm Tree Books, 1976
Frewin, Leslie, *Dietrich*, Frewin, 1967
Greene, Graham, *The Pleasure-Dome*, Secker & Warburg, 1972
Griffith, Richard and Mayer, Arthur, *The Movies*, Spring Books, 1972
Halliwell, Leslie, *The Filmgoer's Companion* (3rd ed.), MacGibbon & Kee, 1970
Kael, Pauline, *Deeper into Movies*, Atlantic; Little Brown, 1973
Kael, Pauline, *Going Steady*, Temple Smith, 1970
Kauffman, Stanley (ed.), *American Film Criticism*, Liveright, 1972
Kobal, John, *Marlene Dietrich*, Studio Vista; Dutton Picturebacks, 1968
Kracauer, Siegfried, *From Caligari to Hitler*, Princeton Press, 1966
Kulik, Karol, *Alexander Korda*, W. H. Allen, 1975

Levin, Martin (ed.), *Hollywood and the Great Fan Magazines*, Ian Allan, 1970

McBride, Joseph, *Orson Welles*, Secker & Warburg, 1972

Madsen, Axel, *Billy Wilder*, Secker & Warburg, 1968

Manvell, Roger, *Love Goddesses of the Movies*, Hamlyn, 1975

Manvell, Roger and Fraenkel, Heinrich, *The German Cinema*, Dent, 1971

Milne, Tom, *Mamoulian*, Thames & Hudson, 1969

Niven, David, *The Moon's a Balloon*, Hamish Hamilton, 1971

Osborne, Robert (ed.), *Academy Awards Illustrated*, Literary Services, 1969

Parish, James Robert, *The Paramount Pretties*, Arlington House, 1972

Picture Show Annual 1937, Howard Barker, 1970

Reed, Rex, *Do You Sleep in the Nude?*, W. H. Allen, 1969

Richards, Jeffrey, *Visions of Yesterday*, Routledge & Kegan Paul, 1973

Robinson, Edward G., *All My Yesterdays*, W. H. Allen, 1974

Rosen, Marjorie, *Popcorn Venus*, Coward, McCann & Geoghegan, 1973

Rotha, Paul, *The Film Till Now*, Spring Books, 1967

Schickel, Richard with Hurlburt, Allen, *The Stars*, Bonanza, 1962

Shipman, David, *The Great Movie Stars—The Golden Years*, Hamlyn, 1970

Springer, John with Hamilton, J. D., *They Had Faces Then*, Citadel, 1974

Sternberg, Josef von, *Morocco/Shanghai Express*, Lorrimer, 1973

Sternberg, Josef von, *The Blue Angel*, Lorrimer, 1968

Sternberg, Josef von, *Fun in a Chinese Laundry*, Secker & Warburg, 1965

Stuart, Ray (ed.), *Immortals of the Screen*, Spring Books, 1967

Thomas, Bob, *Selznick*, W. H. Allen, 1970

Truffaut, François, *Hitchcock*, Secker & Warburg, 1967

Tynan, Kenneth with Beaton, Cecil, *Persona Grata*, Allan Wingate, 1953

Walker, Alexander, *The Celluloid Sacrifice*, Michael Joseph, 1966

Weinberg, Herman G., *Josef von Sternberg*, Dutton, 1967

Weinberg, Herman G., *The Lubitsch Touch*, Dutton, 1968

Weinberg, Herman G., *Saint Cinema*, Drama Book Publishers, 1970

Zinman, David (ed.), *Fifty Classic Motion Pictures*, Crown, 1970

Zukor, Adolph, *The Public is Never Wrong*, Cassell, 1954

For other reference and research material, I am especially indebted to the editors of: *Films and Filming, Films in Review, Picturegoer* and *Picture Show*, and in particular to the following authors:

Bowers, Ronald L., 'Marlene Dietrich 1954–70', *Films in Review*, January 1971

Gow, Gordon, 'Alchemy: Dietrich+Sternberg+German Destiny', *Films and Filming*, June 1974

Knight, Arthur, 'Marlene Dietrich 1923–54', *Films in Review*, December 1954

Whitehall, Richard, 'Dietrich, The Blue Angel', *Films and Filming*, October 1962

Index

personality of, 32, 36, 39, 51, 74, 79, 108; relationship with von Sternberg, 26, 31–2, 36, 51, 54, 58, 63–4, 65–8; Second World War work of, 7, 92–8; sensual appeal, 13, 41, 42, 49, 58, 71, 89; as a singer, 11, 12, 13, 27; theatrical training, 16–17; tour of Britain 1973, 111; Universal Pictures contract with, 87; voice, 8–10, 31, 93
Dishonoured, 49–51, 79
Donat, Robert, 82
Douglas, Melvyn, 84
Dresser, Louise, 64
Du Barry von Heute, Eine, 18
Dunning, Philip, 19

Edinburgh International Festival 1964, 13
Es Liegt in der Luft, 19

Fairbanks, Douglas, Jr, 74
'Falling in Love Again', 8, 27, 107
Farewell to Arms, A, 58
Fesling, Wilhelmina Elizabeth Josephine, *see* Losch, Wilhelmina von
Flame of New Orleans, The, 91
Follow the Boys, 91
Foreign Affair, A, 98
Freudlose Gasse, Die, 18
From Caligari to Hitler, 31
Furthman, Jules, 55

Gabin, Jean, 98
Garbo, Greta, 18, 35, 36, 39, 42, 43, 51, 63, 64
Garden of Allah, The, 74–82
Garmes, Lee, 10, 41, 51, 58
Gershwin, George, 11
Gilbert, John, 71–4
Gloria Palast Theater, Berlin, 34
'Go 'Way From My Window', 107
Golden Earrings, 98
Grand Hotel, 58
Grant, Cary, 60
Grosse Bariton, Der, 17

Halliday, John, 71
Happy Mother, The, 18
Helm, Brigit, 24
Hemingway, Ernest, 13, 108, 112
Hesterberg, Trude, 24
Heston, Charlton, 105
Hitchcock, Alfred, 98
Hollander, Friedrich (Frederick), 11, 31, 87
Hotel Imperial, 74

'I Can't Give You Anything But Love, Baby', 107
'I just can't help it', 8
I Loved a Soldier see *Hotel Imperial*
'I Wish You Love', 12, 13, 107
Ich Küsse Ihre Hand, Madame, 21, 35

Jaffe, Sam, 64
Jannings, Emil, 17, 23–4, 26, 27, 31, 32
Jigsaw, 98
'Jonny', 11, 87, 107
Judgement at Nuremburg, 105

Kismet, 18, 91
Klein Napoleon, Der, 17
Knight Without Armour, 18, 74, 82–4
Korda, Alexander, 18–19, 74
Kracauer, Siegfried, 27–31, 45
Kramer, Stanley, 105
Krauss, Werner, 18

Lady Is Willing, The, 91
Land, Robert, 19
Lang, Fritz, 17, 100
Last Command, The, 23
'Laziest Gal in Town', 8, 98, 107
Leigh, Janet, 105
Liebmann, Robert, 24, 31
Lied ist Aus, Das, 107
'Lili Marlene', 8, 92, 98, 111
Loder, John, 19
Lodge, John, 64
Loesser, Frank, 12, 87
'Lola', 8, 11, 13, 27, 107, 111
Lomas, Herbert, 82
Losch, Edouard von, 15
Losch, Wilhelmina von, 15, 16
Losch, Elisabeth von, 15, 92, 93
Lubitsch, Ernst, 17, 65, 71, 84

McLaglen, Victor, 49
Madame Wünscht Keine Kinder, 19
Mamoulian Rouben, 63
Mann, Heinrich, 24, 27
Mannheim, Lucie, 24, 26
Manon Lescaut, 18, 19
Manpower, 89
'Marie Marie', 12, 13
Marshall, Herbert, 60, 84
Martin Roumagnac, 98
Massine, Greta, 24
May, Joe, 17
Menjou, Adolphe, 41
Mensch am Wege, Der, 18
Merkel, Una, 89